KU-773-796

THE 10
LAWS OF
LEADERSHIP

Dedicated to the Reverend Neville Abrahams who
has always modelled for me the principals contained
in this book.

© 1994 Bill Newman
2nd printing
All Rights Reserved

Published by
BNC Publications
P.O. Box 195
Toowong Qld 4066
Australia

1. THE LEADER HAS VISION

2. THE LEADER HAS DISCIPLINE

3. THE LEADER HAS WISDOM

4. THE LEADER HAS COURAGE

5. THE LEADER HAS HUMILITY

6. THE LEADER IS A DECISION MAKER

7. THE LEADER DEVELOPS FRIENDSHIPS

8. THE LEADER EXERCISES TACT AND DIPLOMACY

9. THE LEADER DEVELOPS EXECUTIVE ABILITY

10. THE LEADER EXUDES INSPIRATIONAL POWER

# THIS BOOK CAN CHANGE YOUR LIFE!

Often when reading a book we decide to apply what we read to our lives. All too often, weeks later, we have forgotten our good intentions. Here are 5 practical ways of ...

## TURNING GOOD INTENTIONS INTO PRACTICAL HABITS.

### 1. USE CARDS

Write out the principles or passages you want to memorise on 3" x 5" cards and review them often.

### 2. MARK YOUR CALENDAR

Mark your calendar daily for the time when you will review your good intentions.

### 3. RE-READ YOUR UNDERLINES

Underline key portions of this book, then re-read your underlines over and over.

### 4. APPLY THE MATERIAL IMMEDIATELY

There is an old saying:
Hear something - you forget it,
See something - you remember it, and
Do something - you understand it.
Apply what you learn as soon as you possibly can - it helps you understand and remember it.

### 5. PRIORITISE WHAT YOU WANT TO LEARN

Select 1-3 things from the book, apply them faithfully and make them a habit. Remember, every person alive struggles with turning their good intentions into habits. Using these 5 points will turn wishing into doing.

INTRODUCTION

—

Leading to
success in a
changing
world

LEADING TO
SUCCESS IN A
CHANGING
WORLD

It has been a great privilege for me over the past several years to mix and mingle with many men and women in numerous areas of society who are leaders. It has always been a fascination as I observe their lives to see just why people would want to follow their leadership.

If ever there was a time in history when we should be studying the principles of leadership it is now. Worldwide we are facing a leadership crisis.

The great need of the hour is for positive, constructive, dynamic, creative and effective leadership.

Business, industry, government, labour, education, and the church are all starving for effective leadership. We may have many people filling administrative positions but the need is for true leaders who are able to do the job more effectively.

Every nation needs to continuously develop leadership skills in order to accomplish success. The world is divided into leaders and followers. Civilization must experience progress, and progress depends upon leadership.

When viewed from a distance, leadership looks so easy. True leaders know only too well that their skills and abilities were developed over an extended period of time.

## WHAT MAKES A GOOD LEADER?

John W. Gardner, former Secretary of the U.S. Department of Health, Education, and Welfare, who is now directing a leadership study project in Washington D.C., has pinpointed five characteristics that set "leader" managers apart from run-of-the-mill managers:

They are long-term thinkers who see beyond the day's crisis and the quarterly report.

Their interest in the company does not stop with the unit they are heading. They want to know how all of the company's departments affect one another, and they are constantly reaching beyond their specific area of influence.

They put heavy emphasis on vision, values and motivation.
They have strong people skills.
They don't accept the status quo. ["Success Magazine"]
What is leadership? Here are a few definitions:

*"A leader is one who guides and develops the activities of others and seeks to provide continual training and direction."*
Ted Engstrom

*"Leadership is the discipline of deliberately exerting special influence within a group to move it toward goals of beneficial permanence that fulfill the group's real needs."*
John Haggai

*"Leadership is:*
*\* Knowing what to do next;*
*\* Knowing why that's important; and*
*\* Knowing how to bring appropriate resources to bear on the need at hand."*
Bobb Biehl

*"Leading is causing people to take effective action."*
Howard Hendricks

Or just to keep it simple:
   A leader is one who knows the way,
   goes the way,
   and shows the way.

Leadership is an awesome responsibility. I have endeavoured in this book to get rid of fuzzy thinking about leadership. Here are ten principles that I believe will see your effectiveness as a leader soar. I trust that they will help you to rise to your full potential. Note that they are principles. You will have to take the time to develop your own steps of action whether or not you lead many or just a few.

The world is full of opportunities waiting to be seized. Be the leader you were meant to be. Be yourself, but be your best self. Dream your dreams, get your pen and paper to develop a plan of action to achieve your goals. Have the courage to act on your ideas despite the possibility of pain, tears and failure. There are risks involved when you say yes to life and decide to reach for goals that you never dreamed possible.

Since creation, billions of people have walked on the earth. There has, and never will be, another one just like you. You are so unique. And because you are so unique you can develop those special talents and abilities you have to fulfill your purpose and destiny.

No matter what happens in this world there will be room at the top and there will always be room for the pioneer.

Become the leader you were meant to be.

**1. THE LEADER HAS VISION**

Dynamic
leadership is
always fired
by vision.

**I. THE LEADER HAS VISION**

"The empires of the future are the empires of the mind." Winston Churchill

Vision is the key to understanding leadership. Without vision you are just playing games with your life. Men and women with vision see more and further than others. Leaders have empires in their brains.

Your imagination is one of the most powerful things you possess. Imagination is your dream machine. Leaders organize special dream times. Time to dream big dreams. The tragedy today is that we crush the ability of our children to dream by demanding that they grow up too soon. Real leaders have never lost that childlike ability to dream dreams.

Helen Keller, that wonderful blind and deaf person, said: "The greatest tragedy to befall a person is to have sight but lack vision".

### IT IS SO TRUE THAT POOR EYES LIMIT A MAN'S SIGHT; POOR VISION, HIS DEEDS.

There is nothing that excites and motivates people like a vision to accomplish something special. Leadership is that special and unique ability to influence people to move toward goals that are beneficial and meet the group's best interests.

Leadership is:

Knowing what to do next;
Knowing why that's important; and
Knowing how to bring appropriate resources to bear on the need at hand.

Strong leadership of a vision, coupled with prayer and faith is an almost unbeatable combination. Confusion on leadership of the vision will result in diminished accomplishments. The vision along with the leadership must be clear and concise.

There was a study done of concentration camp survivors. What were the common characteristics of those who did not succumb to disease and starvation in the camps? Victor Frankl was a living answer to that question. He was a successful Viennese psychiatrist before the Nazis threw him into such a camp. "There is only one reason", he said in a speech, "why I am here today. What kept me alive was you. Others gave up hope. I dreamed. I dreamed that someday I would be here, telling you how I, Victor Frankl, had survived the Nazi concentration camps. I've never been here before, I've never seen any of you before, I've never given this speech before. But in my dreams, I have stood before you and said these words a thousand times."

Study great leaders and you will find they have been dreamers.

*"When you cease to dream, you cease to live."*
Malcolm S. Forbes

Start dreaming and keep on dreaming. If your dream ever gets foggy, set some time aside to resharpen your vision. Have a dream worth dreaming. Most of us have vast potential that has never been developed, simply because we failed to recognise it, or the circumstances in our life have never required it.

In observing leaders over the years, I have often asked myself:
Does the man make the dream?
Or does the dream make the man?
My conclusion is that both are equally true.

The company which doesn't commit at least a small percentage of its time to simply reflect and see new possibilities is doomed to maintaining the status quo.

Take some quality time aside then ask yourselves:
"As a team, what must we do to prepare for the challenges of the next twenty years?" Your vision or dream is simply your view of what life would be like if certain current needs were met. Your

dreams are like a huge motivational magnet. They help pull you through life's low points.

Constantly dare to dream not only personally, but also on the team level. If you want your life and those you work with to be vital in the future, spend time letting your imagination soar.

If you had anything you wanted - unlimited time, unlimited money, unlimited information, unlimited wisdom, unlimited staff - all the resources you could ask for - what would you do? Your answer to that question is your dream.

Vision is a comprehensive sense of where you are, where you are going, how you are going to get there, and what you will do after you get there. It is dreaming dreams about the future. It is seeing the big picture and personally painting a part of it.

Vision is feeling challenged by the world around and being compelled to make a mark on it through the force of your own ideas, personality, resources and desires.

Vision must be focused. If it is too broad people will flounder and become discouraged. If it is non-specific, it is useless. It must be clear, concise and in focus. Blurry vision causes people to lose their way.

Without limiting the vision, at the same time it must be attainable. Set realistic reachable goals otherwise you will become discouraged and will discourage others.

"There was a cartoon recently showing two Eskimos sitting on chairs, fishing through holes in the ice. The one on the right was sitting with his line in a hole about the size of a small manhole. The Eskimo on the left was also sitting with his line in the water. His hole, however, reached almost to the end of the lake. It was about the size and shape of a whale.

"Now that is vision. He is thinking big. How do you think the other Eskimo felt sitting next to this guy with the big hole? My guess is that every now and again he looked over and wondered if he should cut his hole bigger. Vision is contagious. It may look foolish but it can have a profound effect on others." [1]

So much of what we undertake lacks vision. We cut our tiny holes in the ice and make our plans to go home cold and hungry.

You may have heard of the shoe salesman that went to Africa and contacted his manufacturer back home, "I want to come home. Nobody wears shoes in this part of the world. So they brought him back home and then sent out another salesman who shipped back order after order. He wrote to the home office, "Everybody here needs shoes!" Now that's seeing the glass half full or half empty.

Napoleon saw Italy, but not the Alps. He had an objective and he knew where he was going. Washington saw the Hessians at Trenton. A man of smaller stature would have seen the Delaware choked with ice.

The majority see the obstacles; the few see the objectives. Obstacles are what you see when you take your eyes off the goals.

To the Israelites, Goliath was "too big to hit"; but to little David, he was "too big to miss".

Vision is the blazing campfire around which people will gather. It provides light, energy, warmth and unity, but many of us stand away in the shadows and refuse to come up to the fire and be part of the vision.

In 1886, the U.S. Patent Office was very nearly closed because some congressmen didn't want to include it in the budget. One Congressman said, "It now appears that everything practical has already been invented." That was before telephones, computors, cars, airplanes, and a million other inventions.

We need visionaries, who will embark on high-risk ventures. History is full of them and we are the better for it today. It's people who have vision. Programmes don't have vision. All too often we take the spirit out of visionaries.

Vision starts very much out of attitude and attitude determines altitude. What dreams and visions keep you awake at night? What fresh idea would revolutionize your life? How can you develop this idea so that others will get excited about joining you in changing your world?

Forget the cynics and the knockers. They will always be around in abundance to knock you. There will always be the discouragers and the doubters who can't see beyond the first obstacle. People of vision are not afraid to fail.

*"The tragedy of life is not that we die, but what dies inside a man while he lives."*
Albert Schweitzer

A leader is one that has the courage to dream, the ability to organize, and the strength to execute the action necessary. A leader is simply one who knows where they want to go, gets up and goes.

*"Neither you nor the world knows what you can do until you have tried."*
Ralph Waldo Emerson

## NOTICE THREE VITAL THINGS ABOUT VISION

1. Vision creates power. The enthusiasm that comes from vision results in dynamic power. This then leads to greater productivity and feelings of productivity increase your feelings of self-esteem. Enthusiasm is produced from vision and the

power from enthusiasm is the energy that drives every successful idea.

2. Great vision comes from being quiet, still, often alone. Every leader needs to spend time in solitude and reflection. We live in a crazy rat-race world. Find a place where you can enjoy solitude. In a quiet place will come your best ideas.

3. Never allow your vision to escape you. Just as a fire will die without fuel so too will your visions and dreams unless you keep them constantly alive. Your vision should be so much part of you that you are living it day by day. Each day you need to rehearse and go over your vision. Visions rebuild themselves in quietness, not in the hustle and bustle of life.

*"We grow by dreams. All big men are dreamers. Some of us let dreams die, but others nourish and protect them, nurse them through bad days... to the sunshine and light which always comes."*
Woodrow Wilson

●●●

## VISION

### VISION HAS NO FORCE, POWER OR IMPACT UNLESS IT SPREADS FROM THE VISIONARY TO THE VISIONLESS.

"A mark of a great leader is the ability not only to capture the vision, but also to articulate it and to cause people to fully embrace it. Because vision concerns action, it is imperative that the vision be cast in such a way that people understand and can respond to it. Vision is not to be jealously guarded, a perspective to be protected. For the vision to have impact, it must be a shared vision." [Adapted from "The Power of Vision" by George Barna]

# VISION

Vision is the basis for your success.

Vision is essential for leaders. You will see further down the track than your peers. You'll know where you're going.

Vision creates goals that you set for yourself. They become the motivating factors to continually drive you out of complacency. They help you overcome failure and hardship.

Vision moves you to capture the dream God has put in your heart. Vision never allows you the luxury of discourgement. It never allows you to accept anything that is negative.

Vision challenges you to implement many goals that will accomplish your dreams.

BUT.... It all starts with you having a VISION.

## THE IMPORTANCE OF VISION AND GOALSETTING

Goals are vision with feet. Goals are a set of specific, measurable steps to achieve the vision. When realistic goals are set and met, you will feel satisfied and successful. The whole concept of setting goals will have the exciting flavour of accomplishment. Goal setting will deliver you from crisis management. You switch from fire fighting to fire prevention.

Goal setting will help you to constantly resharpen your vision. An axeman never loses time sharpening his axe. Take time to hone and rehone your goals.

Henry Kaisor said, "Determine what you want more than anything else in life, write down the means by which you intend to attain it, and permit nothing to deter you from pursuing it."

Here are some questions that may help you to establish some long range goals over the next ten years:

1. What do I want to do?
2. What do I want to be?
3. What do I want to see?
4. What do I want to have?
5. Where do I want to go?
6. What would I like to share?

Here are some of the benefits of goalsetting:

1. Goals simplify the decision-making process.

The leader is constantly faced with a multitude of decisions. Invitations to join this Board or that, to speak at conventions and meetings, a thousand and one opportunities come. Their gift makes way for them. Others feel they can organize your life better than you can. When you know your direction in life as you establish goals so you can evaluate simply and easily each situation as it presents itseif.

2. Goals tone up mental and physical health.

The reason so many people die soon after retirement is that they have ceased to set goals for themselves. Without direction in your life you are vulnerable to negative thought patterns. It is well known that your mental attitude and your physical health are closely related. Having set goals will demand that you keep sharp, mentally and physically in shape.

3. Goals generate respect.

People admire and respect someone who knows where they are going. During his days as President, Thomas Jefferson and a group of companions were travelling across the country on horseback. They came to a river which had left its banks because of a recent downpour. The swollen river had washed the bridge away. Each rider was forced to ford the river on horseback, fighting for his life against the rapid currents. The very real possibility of death threatened each rider, which caused a traveller who was not part of their group to step aside and watch. After several had plunged in and made it to the other side, the stranger asked President Jefferson if he would ferry him across the river. The President agreed without hesitation. The man climbed on, and shortly thereafter the two of them made it safely to the other side. As the stranger slid off the back of the saddle onto dry land, one in the group asked him, "Tell me, why did you select the President to ask this favour of?" The man was shocked, admitting he had no idea it was the President who had helped him. "All I know," he said, "is that on some of your faces were written the answer 'No' and on some of your faces the answer was 'Yes'. His was a 'Yes' face." [2]

Those with goals have a 'Yes' face. They inspire others to greater heights. As I walked through the basement which served as the War Cabinet rooms for Winston Churchill during the Second World War's dark days, I reflected on his tenacity under tremendous pressure to lead a nation at war. His goals for England generated the respect needed to lead his nation.

4. Goals help you to realize and enjoy the feeling of accomplishment. What you cannot measure, you cannot monitor. Without goals you float aimlessly, but as you achieve your goals there is a feeling of satisfaction and accomplishment.

5. Goals produce persistence.

Persistence or staying power is the quality that sets the leader apart. Just as the stamp sticks to the letter until it gets there, so the leader never gives up.

Problems and discouragements will face the leader, but he can overcome them with staying power.

The bee has been aptly described as "busy". To produce one kilogram of honey, the bee must visit 56,000 clover heads. Since each flower head has 60 flower tubes, a total of 3,360,000 visits are necessary to give us that kilogram of honey for our breakfast table. Meanwhile the worker bee has flown the equivalent of three times around the world. Talk about persistence!

Many times we are nearer our goals than we think we are so never give up - persist. It's always too soon to quit.

6. Goals deliver the leader from the deception and desire for applause. Leaders become unstuck when they start to believe their own publicity! It's always a fact of life that a third of the crowd care for you, a third of the crowd don't care for you and the other third couldn't care less about you! That should bring you down to earth.

Goals deliver you from living in the past. A leader, often because of his hard work, will receive justified praise. The problem arises when his ego needs to feed on it.

Having set goals the leader takes his mind off the past and centres his attention on the future.

## GOALSETTING IS AN ONGOING DISCIPLINE

Thomas Edison set himself an ambitious goal. It was to come up with a major new invention every six months, a minor invention every ten days. When he died he had 1,092 US patents and over 2,000 foreign ones.

Edison knew that by setting such goals for himself, and striving to reach them, he was bound to increase his output. The same principle applies, no matter what goals you set for yourself, they are bound to help your results. Challenge yourself - then rise to meet that challenge.

Goals and plans are the keys to achievement and success. Only 3% of people have goals and write them down; 10% more have goals and plans, but keep them in their heads. The rest - 87% - drift through life without definite goals or plans. They do not know where they are going and let others dictate to them.

The 3% who have goals and plans that are written down accomplish from 50 to 100 times more during their lifetime than the 10% who have goals and plans but merely keep them in their heads.

So -
(1) Set definite goals.
(2) Establish a plan of action for their fulfillment.
(3) Commit your goals and plans to writing within a specific time frame.

## THE FEAR OF GOALSETTING

With all the advantages of goalsetting, why is it that so many balk at taking the time to establish even the simplest goals for their life? A primary reason is simply - fear.

1. There is the fear of imperfect goals.

Some fear their goals will not work out so they are afraid to set targets and make advance plans.

2. The fear of defeat.

You will never reach a distant shore if you are afraid of losing sight of the harbour. Yes, there is a real possibility that you will end up flat on your face, but what a tragedy if you never attempt anything important or vital with your life.

"Attempt something so great that it is doomed for failure, unless God be in it." John Haggai.

Be ashamed to die until you achieve something great for God.

3. The fear of ridicule.

We are always worried about what they will think - but who are they? The fear of man does bring a snare, as the Bible says. If your knees are knocking... kneel on them.

If you are in the front line, you will be the first to be shot at! There will always be the cynics and the knockers. They mocked Noah as he built the ark. Check any park. There has never been a statue erected to a cynic. There was a sign on a door, "Come in without knocking, go out the same way." If you throw mud you lose ground!

It is important to listen to sound and good advice from a trusted source but don't allow yourself to be distracted fearing the reaction of others.

4. The fear of thinking goalsetting as presumptious.

If leaders considered their backgrounds, education or qualifications for their task in hand, there would have been very little attempted in this world.

Mark Twain said, "If you think you can or you think you can't, you're probably right."

Nothing is impossible to the willing heart. Progress results from persistence with purpose.

Keep your eyes on your goals and you will forget about yourself. The person that has accomplished all he/she thinks is worthwhile has begun to die.

Let faith, not fear guide your life.

## THE IMPORTANCE OF GOALSETTING

John Haggai in his book "Lead On", talks about S-M-A-R-T goals. He says to make your goals:

Specific - Each goal must be a specific step rather than a vague desire.

Measurable - If you can't measure it, you can't monitor it.

Attainable - goals, but not unattainable ones.

Realistic - State what results can be realistically achieved, given your available resources.

Tangible - Making your goals tangible is the only realistic way of achieving intangible goals. [3]

## THE ADVANTAGES OF GOALSETTING

The establishment of a goals' programme is the way you can fulfill your vision. Setting goals is not a one-time exercise. It is an ongoing discipline. Without a goals' programme, a vision is only wishful thinking. Your goals will have to be constantly modified. While you are working on your immediate or short range goals, you must be careful to keep your eyes on your long range goals.

Your vision must remain permanent but your goals must remain flexible. Do not change the order. Far too many churches, businesses, teaching institutions and individual lives allow their vision to change and make their goals permanent. So often it starts with a man, then it becomes a movement, then a machine, then just a monument to the glory of past things.

A leader must have a vision, but that vision must be fulfilled by goals that work toward the achievement of the vision. A vision is the foundation for all leadership. But where the rubber meets the road is with a set of specific, measurable steps or goals to achieve the vision.

A leader has one life-dominating vision which he converts to a life-compelling mission. But his goals are many. A vision must be broad enough to be permanent. Goals will change and develop.

## HOW TO SET GOALS TO ACHIEVE YOUR MASTERPLAN

When realistic goals are set and met, you will feel successful, and the whole concept of setting goals will have the exciting flavour of accomplishment.

Charles Schwaab was given a million dollars for this simple piece of advice:

1. Make a list.
2. Put priorities in order.
3. Do the list.

Not bad for a million dollars but it made billions.

Goals are critical for success and achievement. Here are some simple steps to help you to develop your goal setting programme:

1. Set time aside where you can do some undisturbed dreaming. The world's greatest area of undeveloped territory lies beneath people's hats! It was the great Benjamin Disraeli who said, "Nurture your mind with great thoughts, for you never go any higher than you think." If you want to become successful you must think until it hurts. Most are mentally lazy by nature. Train

your mind to think and to dream again. Your mind is like a muscle. It must be exercised to grow.

Children are able to fantasize. Their dreams are so vivid. We have to continually develop the ability to dream. Find a quiet place and dream again.

Begin by outlining a clearly defined picture of what you want to BE, DO, HAVE or HELP in twenty years time.

Work backwards from twenty years, ten years, five years, three years, and one year.

The areas should include:
1. Financial
2. Family
3. Friends
4. Associations or groups you are involved with
5. Emotional
6. Physical
7. Career
8. Spiritual

This is the time to let your mind soar. Make sure you have plenty of unhurried time. This place of quiet is where you must return to continually. If you do not take control of your thought life, you will be a slave of your surroundings.

If you want to be successful you must think, think, think! Very little can stand against the pressure of sustained thought and brainstorming. Every great achiever will acknowledge that they could have done more or gone further.

Take time to think, it is the source of power.

Dreams do come true, if you dare to dream.

It's like the old song says, "If you don't have a dream, how you gonna make a dream come true?"

2. Develop your masterplan.

It is time to put pen to paper.

No matter how far out they may seem, start writing your dreams down on a paper pad or notebook. Work over the eight areas mentioned earlier [You may have more to add]. Let your mind soar. Don't restrict yourself. Forget about the opinions of others. At this time you must be completely alone away from the television, radio, telephone, people and any other distractions. This is the time to really mean business.

In our action-oriented society we are more attuned to action rather than contemplation. With all the noise, hustle and bustle of a busy rat race existence, it is important to develop the ability to stop and dream.

Before a painter starts work on a masterpiece, he has to spend some time designing the painting. You are wanting your life to count. To do so will take planning.

But this is just the broad brush stage. The details will come later when you work on your action plan.

A masterplan is simply a written statement that clearly defines your forward planning, your direction, your organization, and your resources.

The conductor has the complete musical score while each musician has his individual part to play. The site forman has the master blueprint and each tradesman has his individual drawings.

Your masterplan will crystallize your visions and dreams.

You now have a vision, it is time now to sharpen the focus of your vision. Your vision is the foundation for all leadership. Having a vision now requires a commitment to action. This is the time to create your masterplan.

Now you begin to bring all the wild ideas, your dreams and visions together in some systematic form.

The vision will stay the same over a long period of time and your masterplan will correspond to the vision. Your goals, however, will have to be reviewed often and revised in order to adjust them to changing situations in order to realize your vision.

At this stage you should be working on your mission statement for you personally, your team, association and Board of Directors. On a personal level the question is, "Why do I exist?" Or on a group level, "Why does this organization, this business exist?" It is like your North Star, it is there to give you direction and keep you on track. It answers the question, "What is my purpose?"

At this stage you will have to ask yourself some pertinent questions:

1. Assess the needs you will have to meet.
   (The business world calls it their market.)
2. What team do I need to accomplish the dream?
3. What advisors do I need to succeed?
   (Committees, expertise, Directors)
4. Determine the direction.
5. Organize responsibility. (The right people in the right place.)
6. How much will it cost? (Develop a projected budget.)

You may need to develop a flow chart of your operation no matter how big or small.

As your support team grows there are five areas that you will have to carefully monitor:

1. Reporting
   This is the way you check you are on target. As a leader you are responsible for helping your team achieve their goals - goals which you and they have agreed on.

2. Communication
   Develop an effective method of keeping everyone in touch.

3. Evaluating
   People, programme, progress, organization, and quality all need to be evaluated.

4. Refining
   Continually ask, "How can we do it better?"
   As well as the time you set aside yourself to develop and define your vision, spend time with your associates and work as a team effort. This will encourage a group's team spirit.

5. Develop your action plan
   This is the important stage where you develop your set of specific, measurable steps to achieve your vision.

The vision is important, but the vision will never be realized unless a goals' programme is put in place and faithfully followed. Goalsetting is not easy, and it takes constant review and change. Without a goals' programme, the vision is merely wishful thinking. Goalsetting should be second nature to the leader.

You should have measurable goals in each of your objective areas. Be careful not to set too many or you will be overwhelmed. As you reach these goals you will feel successful. If you don't reach them you will not feel as successful. But remember - you don't have to reach them all to make a major difference. You can do extremely significant things if you reach only half your goals.

Keep your goals in balance. Balance is the key to living. For example, you don't sacrifice your family for the sake of unrealistic goals.

Your action plan should list the specific steps you expect to take and when. You should put all these steps in writing. Your action plan is not something you produce and file away in a drawer, it must be constantly referred to, adjusted or modified.

## SETTING YOUR GOALS FOR SUCCESS

It has been well said that a definite purpose is the starting point for all achievement. You have to know what you want and how you are going to achieve it. Let me now give you some stepping stones to help you achieve your dreams through goal planning.

1. Form a very specific, clear picture of what you want.
   Our problem is that we have too much muddy thinking. It takes time and effort to crystallize our goals. Sometimes we have to think until it hurts. Sometimes it demands quality and quantity time. Good ideas are like gold and jewels, they have to be mined. Nothing can hold against the attack of sustained thought.

I heard about a church that was to build a new sanctuary. When the plans were complete the Church leaders, instead of just handing them over to the builders, took them away for the weekend and spent time visualizing and thinking them through. They imagined themselves walking up to the front door in the daytime. Then someone thought what it would be like at night and realized that the control light switches were a long way from the front door, a hopeless situation at night. Others noticed that as soon as they walked through the front door, instead of entering a beautifully appointed foyer, all they could see was an ugly fire hydrant on the wall. Room after room was dealt with in this way until ultimately they saved themselves many thousands of dollars.

Dreaming, visualizing, getting a clear specific picture is a very profitable exercise both in time and money.

### SPEND TIME GETTING A CLEAR PICTURE OF WHAT YOU WANT TO ACCOMPLISH.

2. Determine whether or not you are prepared to pay the price. There is no gain without pain. So many often come to a desperation quotient before they are prepared to do something. They may be disgusted at the slave trade like Wilberforce. They may get mad at segregation like Martin Luther King. They may be infuriated at the porn plague like Mary Whitehouse. They may be heartbroken over the poor like Mother Teresa. Their country may have its back to the wall to move them into action like Winston Churchill. They may be sickened by the profiteering of religion, like Jesus when he drove the racketeers from the temple.

A leader with a burning desire must be prepared to pay a price. Something may have to click inside of you whereby you will get mad enough or determined enough, desperate enough or concerned enough or for some other reason you will endure the pain and pay the price for achievement. It will not be handed to you on a silver plate. You have to pay the price. But remember that if it is easy it is not worth having. If Mount Everest was easy to climb, the challenge would not be there. If the moon was a small plane flight away, the thrill of standing in the moondust would be insignificant.

What are some of the other costs for the price of leadership? There is criticism, fatigue, the effort to think, loneliness, identifying with people, making unpleasant decisions, the effect of competition, the possibility of the abuse of power, false pride and jealousy, time management and rejection.

If you are not willing to pay the price of leadership it is pointless to read on. You will only be playing games with your life. But remember, every worthwhile accomplishment has a price tag in terms of hard work, patience, faith, and endurance.

3. Develop a plan of action.

Every building, no matter how small or great, must start with a blueprint. Your life, your dreams, your goals, are far more important than any building of brick, concrete, timber or stone. Your life is far more valuable than any man-made structure.

Here are four steps in developing your modus operandi as a leader.

(1) Goals and strategy, including long and short range planning.
(2) Organization. This concerns people and structure.
(3) Implementation. The day-to-day execution of plans.
(4) Persistence. Sustained staying power.

It is time now to practically and systematically set out your goals. Remember, goals are a set of specific, measurable steps that design the programme for fulfilling your vision.

1. Make a list of your goals.

Write down all the goals that you can think of in the four areas: Being, Doing, Owning, Accomplishing. Start with 20 years then 15, then 10, then 5, then 1 year, then 6 months, then 90 days, then 60 days.

2. Now rearrange them in order of priority for each of the four areas. Select the goals you want first. Next set a target date. Be realistic. Make them attainable goals. A goal without a deadline is not really a goal....it is a wish.

3. Make a list of the required action you must take to achieve your goal. For example, the extra effort required, or more study, or the cash needed. (Remember, no gain without pain).

4. Develop the qualities in your personal behaviour that will be required. Obtain the skills. For example - a pleasant personality,

neat appearance, mental awareness, a winning smile, a warm handshake, a positive walk or plain hard work.

5. List your deficiencies and conquer them, starting right now! Today!

6. List the personnel or help needed to achieve your goals and the techniques or methods as well.

7. Develop an iron will determination to follow through your plans regardless of obstacles, criticism or circumstances, or what other people say, think or do.

8. Visualise the new you. Vividly imagine yourself as having already reached your goals.

9. Begin at once.

In the absence of clearly defined goals, we are forced to concentrate on activity and ultimately become enslaved by it. Remember, there is no joy in victory without running the risk of defeat.

**OPPORTUNITIES NEVER COME TO THOSE WHO WAIT, THEY ARE CAPTURED BY THOSE WHO DARE TO ATTACK.**

The fulfillment of our goals must be good for others. If they bring harm to others, then our goals are selfish. The great rewards in life are love and achievement. All else is secondary. Become a giver - not a getter.

Don't be afraid to set goals.

To achieve goals demands hard work, determination and commitment. For many though, the main reason they do not establish a quest to achieve goals is plain fear; the fear of ridicule from others or the fear of defeat. Others fear that their goals will not be perfect - or worse still, they may consider themselves presumptuous.

The importance and the benefit of goal setting is immeasurable. Without setting goals your visions and dreams are just wishful thinking. There are so many benefits in goalsetting. They make decisionmaking easier. Your physical and mental health is better. You have established a positive attitude to life. You are helping to eliminate stress, confusion and fear. Those who have goals attract respect from people. It gives you a sense of accomplishment. It gives you "stickability" and staying power. It is staying power that sets the leader apart.

## THE TRAGEDY OF LIFE DOESN'T LIE IN NOT REACHING YOUR GOAL; THE TRAGEDY LIES IN HAVING NO GOAL TO REACH.

Henry Kaiser said, "Determine what you want more than anything else in life, write down the means by which you intend to attain it, and permit nothing to deter you from pursuing it."

Without goals and priorities we will never escape the tyranny of the urgent. If we do not have our eye fixed on a goal, the urgent will crowd out the important.

The only difference between being a "dreamer" and a "goalsetter" is adding a deadline to the dream.

Goalsetting accomplishes your vision.

4. Mission Statement.
    To keep you on course with a clarity of purpose, set aside some extended time to prepare a succinct, personal and organisational mission statement.

A mission statement focuses your energies and lets you enjoy a sense of direction and purpose. It prevents you from being distracted and sidetracked. It also focuses your personal energies and resources. You don't spend time, money and effort on things that don't bring return and are not related to your purpose for living.

Use your mission statement to direct and unify your life. A constant reaching of your mission statement will help in keeping yourself motivated. Your mission statement should be such that it is a constant challenge to you.

### PLANNING IS 80% THINKING AND 20% WRITING - THEN 100% DOING!

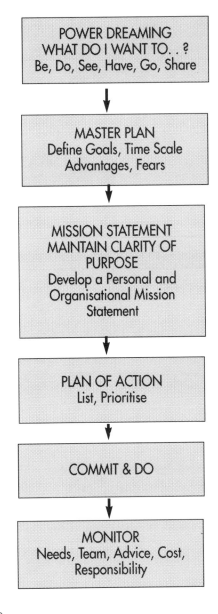

**VISION PLANNING**

POWER DREAMING
WHAT DO I WANT TO. . ?
Be, Do, See, Have, Go, Share

↓

MASTER PLAN
Define Goals, Time Scale
Advantages, Fears

↓

MISSION STATEMENT
MAINTAIN CLARITY OF
PURPOSE
Develop a Personal and
Organisational Mission
Statement

↓

PLAN OF ACTION
List, Prioritise

↓

COMMIT & DO

↓

MONITOR
Needs, Team, Advice, Cost,
Responsibility

**2.THE
LEADER HAS
DISCIPLINE**

Nothing
worthwhile
or significant
is possible
without
discipline.

## 2. THE LEADER HAS DISCIPLINE

Continual success cannot be achieved without discipline.

Self-discipline is - "the willingness to perform the acts that are beneficial to us that - for whatever reason - we don't want to perform".

"Discipline is the basic set of tools we require to solve life's problems. Without discipline we can solve nothing. With only some discipline we can solve only some problems. With total discipline we can solve all problems." [Scott Peck - The Road Less Travelled]

Some regard discipline as hardship. In reality it permits success and sets you free from futile living.

**IN THIS WORLD WE EITHER DISCIPLINE OURSELVES OR WE ARE DISCIPLINED BY OTHERS.**

Discipline is required of the athlete to win the game. Discipline is required for the captain running his ship. Discipline is needed for the pianist to practise for the concert. Discipline is vital for the student to pass that exam. Discipline is mandatory for leaders to achieve their goals and dreams.

One of the great failures of our generation has been to underestimate the importance of discipline. Influenced by a superficial psychology, we have abhorred restraint, indulged our natural impulses and crucified inhibitions. We forget too easily that no worthwhile or significant life or work is possible without discipline.

Vince Lombardi, the legendary coaching genius who was the only man to ever coach three consecutive world championship football teams once said, "I've never known a man worth his salt who, in the long run, deep down in his heart, did not appreciate the grind and the discipline. There is something in good men that truly yearns for and needs discipline." Lombardi knew that if you wanted something in life you had to plan for it, prepare yourself for it and then, most important, you had to go for it.

There is an old saying that "a thousand wishes won't fill a bucket with fishes".

Thinking and feeling do not produce action. Only action produces thinking and feeling.

Mark Twain put it this way: "Thunder is good; thunder is impressive; but it is the lightning that gets the job done".

## THE LEADER IS A FIGHTER

When the disease of discouragement hits us, all too soon we give up the fight. I remember travelling from Sydney to San Francisco. They were screening the first "Rocky" film. The plane had caught a tailwind and we arrived ten minutes early. The passengers were so cross not knowing how the fight ended! As I read the reviews from the following "Rocky" films, the boxer becomes successful as the heavyweight champion of the world. One night he is watching a video of his next opponent. He sees the fight in his eyes. Fear begins to grip Rocky. He thinks to himself, "This guy can take me." Fortunately his trainer sees what is happening. He takes the fighter back to the smelly back alleys with the leaking taps, back to where he came from and instils the fight back into the champion.

I see this so often among leaders. They reach a certain level of "success" and they plateau. They lose the fight. They need to go back to their roots, back to where they started, back to where it was really tough. They need the fight, the steel put back into their life, the fire back in their belly.

Ted Engstrom writes with insight: "Cripple him, and you have a Sir Walter Scott. Lock him in a prison cell, and you have a John Bunyan. Bury him in the snows of Valley Forge, and you have a

George Washington. Raise him in abject poverty, and you have an Abraham Lincoln. Strike him down with infantile paralysis, and he becomes Franklin Roosevelt. Burn him so severely that the doctors say he'll never walk again, and you have a Glen Cunningham who set the world's one mile record in 1934. Deafen him and you have a Ludwig van Beethoven. Have him or her born black in a society filled with racial discrimination, and you have a Booker T. Washington, a Marian Anderson, a George Washington Carver... Call him a slow learner, 'retarded,' and write him off as uneducatable, and you have an Albert Einstein." [4]

As one man summed it up: Life is about twenty per cent what happens to us and eighty per cent in the way we respond to the events.

Thomas Edison was an amazing character! Thanks to his genius, we enjoy the microphone, the phonograph, the incandescent light, the storage battery, talking movies and more than a thousand other inventions. But beyond all that Edison was a man who refused to be discouraged. His contagious optimism affected all those around him.

His son recalled a freezing December night in 1914. Unfruitful experiments on the nickel-iron-alkaline storage battery, a 10 year project, had put Edison on a financial tightrope. He was still solvent only because of profits from movie and record production.

On that December evening the cry "fire!" echoed through the plant. Spontaneous combustion had broken out in the film room. Within minutes all the packing compounds, celluloid for records and film and other flammable goods were burning. Fire companies from eight surrounding towns arrived, but the heat was so intense and the water pressure so low that attempts to douse the flames were futile. Everything was being destroyed.

When he couldn't find his father, the son became concerned. Was he safe? With all his assets being destroyed, would his spirit be broken? Soon he saw his father in the plant yard running toward him.

"Where's Mom?" shouted the inventor. "Go get her, son! Tell her to hurry up and bring her friends! They'll never see a fire like this again!"

Early the next morning, long before dawn, with the fire barely under control, Edison called his employees together and made an incredible announcement. "We're rebuilding!"

He told one man to lease all the machine shops in the area. He told another to obtain a wrecking crane from the Erie Railroad Company. Then, almost as an afterthought, he added, "Oh, by the way, anybody know where we can get some money?"

Later he explained, "We can always make capital out of a disaster. We've just cleared out a bunch of old rubbish. We'll build bigger and better on the ruins". Shortly after that, he yawned, rolled up his coat for a pillow, curled up on a table and immediately fell asleep.

Harold Sherman, quite a while ago, wrote a book entitled "How to Turn Failure into Success". In it he gives a "Code of Persistence". If you give up too easily, write this down and read it daily.

1. I will never give up as long as I know I am right.
2. I will believe that all things will work out for me if I hang on until the end.
3. I will be courageous and undismayed in the face of odds.
4. I will not permit anyone to intimidate me or deter me from my goals.
5. I will fight to overcome all physical handicaps and setbacks.
6. I will try again and again and yet again to accomplish what I desire.
7. I will take new faith and resolution from the knowledge that all successful men and women had to fight defeat and adversity.

8. I will never surrender to discouragement or despair no matter what seeming obstacles may confront me.

A page from John Wesley's Diary reads as follows:

> Sunday morning, May 5, preached in St. Ann's, was asked not to come back anymore.
> Sunday p.m., May 5, preached at St. John's, deacons said "Get out and stay out".
> Sunday a.m., May 12, preached at St. Jude's, can't go back there either.
> Sunday p.m., May 12, preached at St. George's, kicked out again.
> Sunday a.m., May 19, preached at St. somebody else's, deacons called a special meeting and said I couldn't return.
> Sunday p.m., May 19, preached on the street, kicked off the street.
> Sunday a.m., May 26, preached in meadow, chased out of meadow as a bull was turned loose during the services.
> Sunday a.m., June 2, preached out at the edge of town, kicked off the highway.
> Sunday p.m., June 2, afternoon service, preached in a pasture, 10,000 people came to hear me.

It happened in Southwest Asia in the 14th Century. The army of Asian conqueror Emperor Tamerlane (a descendant of Ghengis Khan) has been routed, dispersed by a powerful enemy. Tamerlane himself lay hidden in a deserted manger while enemy troops scoured the countryside. As he lay there, desperate and dejected, Tamerlane watched an ant try to carry a grain of corn over a perpendicular wall. The kernel was larger than the ant itself. As the emperor counted, sixty-nine times the ant tried to carry it up the wall. Sixty-nine times he fell back. On the seventieth try he pushed the grain of corn over the top.

Tamerlane leaped to his feet with a shout! He, too, would triumph in the end! And he did, reorganizing his forces and putting the enemy to flight.

For Michael J. Coles, every day is a comeback. A devastating motorcycle accident taught him the most important lesson of his life - You must always surpass your goals.

Life was sweet when Coles and a partner launched the Original Great American Chocolate Chip Cookie Co. with $8,000. In the first month, his company pulled in $32,000.

Then it happened. "I was on my way home on my motorcycle", recalls Coles. "I hit a rock and slammed into a telephone pole". He awoke the next morning in the hospital. With three limbs in casts and his face wrapped in bandages, he slowly set about repairing his body and his business.

Coles made what others thought was acceptable progress. One day, though, he was hobbling up his driveway when his daughter challenged him to a race. He tried to run, and then he froze. "I realized I was mentally handicapped too".

Stung by humiliation, Coles took his first real step forward - "I decided that moment that whatever it took I would try to fully recover". He designed an excruciating rehabilitation programme of weight lifting, squatting, and bicycling. "I set an impossible goal - I would become the best bicyclist around".

After four years of training, he bicycled across the country in fifteen and a half days - a new world record. But all Coles could think about was breaking his own record. He did two years later.

Coles also pushed an aggressive franchise plan that has now reached sales of seventy million dollars. "The accident taught me something", Coles muses. "If you get run off the road, you get right up and start over again." [5]

Press on.
Nothing in the world
Can take the place of persistence.

Talent will not;
Nothing is more common
Than unsuccessful men
With talent.
Genius will not;
Unrewarded genius
Is almost a proverb.
Education will not;
The world is full of
Educated derelicts.
Persistence and determination
Alone are important.

The leader will learn to fight against the disease of discouragement, depression and despondency.

## THE LEADER KNOWS HOW TO WORK EFFECTIVELY

Any farmer will tell you that cows do not "give milk", you have to fight for every drop!

True success comes from hard work. There are no short cuts. I'm not talking about a workaholic but rather one who has learnt to enjoy work. So many want to work to get rich so they will not have to work. Most with that attitude never make it anyway.

The key is to work smarter, not harder. (As you begin you will have to work smarter and harder!) You must be constantly thinking, "How can I do this better? Is there a more cost effective way, how can I conserve time, can I produce better doing it a different way?"

Leadership success is having a dream then work, work, work. Learn to love work. There are so many in hospital that would do anything to get out with a healthy body and work. Work is a principle that God has given to man. Even before Adam sinned against God, God placed him in the Garden of Eden to keep it.

Work will always seem harder when it's less enjoyable. It is not work that is a curse but drudgery. Every one of us have things to do we don't like. Real achievers develop the ability to enjoy whatever they do.

What would it be like in a hospital bed, or a wheelchair, or unable to get a job. There are millions right now who would give anything to have and enjoy what you have.

Success is hard work in disguise. Success, work, discipline all go together. There are two types of pain in life, the pain of discipline and the pain of regret. Which would you sooner have?

"Dressed as a rag doll, Melody Schick, 24, sat with a teddy bear cradled in her left arm and staring into space from a revolving platform. Only her eyes moved. Then, five hours and 43 boring minutes later she rose slowly and tried to smile. Miss Schick was seeking to beat the world record for sitting still! The previous record was 5 hours and 32 minutes. The record attempt took place at a Dallas shopping centre as hundreds of shoppers watched." [6]

There are many now who could compete for that record! They have been sitting still - metaphorically, if not literally - for years. They never get involved in work or participate in any programme.

Once upon a time there were four men named Everybody, Somebody, Anybody, and Nobody. There was an important job to be done and Everybody was asked to do it. But Everybody was sure that Somebody would do it. Anybody could have done it. But Nobody did it. Somebody got angry about it, because it was Everybody's job. Everybody thought that Anybody could do it, and Nobody realized that Everybody wouldn't do it. It ended up that Everybody blamed Somebody and Nobody did the job that Anybody could have done in the first place! [Author Unknown]

The old plumber was admonishing his young helper, who was always taking coffee breaks. "When I was an apprentice," he said, "we used to lay the first two lengths of pipe - then the boss would turn on the water and we'd have to stay ahead of it."

## THE DICTIONARY IS THE ONLY PLACE WHERE SUCCESS COMES BEFORE WORK!

"An old farmer who was about to die, called his two sons to his bedside and said, "My boys, my farm and the field are yours in equal shares. I leave you a little ready money but the bulk of my wealth is hidden somewhere in the ground, not more than eighteen inches from the surface. I regret that I've forgotten precisely where it lies". When the old man was dead and buried his two sons set to work to dig up every inch of ground in order to find the buried treasure. They failed to find it but as they had gone to all the trouble of turning over the soil they thought they might as well sow a crop, which they did, reaping a good harvest. In autumn as soon as they had opportunity, they dug for the treasure again with no better results. As their fields were turned over more thoroughly than any others in the area they reaped better harvests than anyone else. Year after year their search continued. Only when they had grown much older and wiser did they realize what their father had meant. Real treasure comes as a result of hard work." [7]

A student once wrote to the famous preacher Henry Ward Beecher, asking him how to obtain "an easy job". Mr Beecher replied, "If that's your attitude, you'll never amount to anything. You cannot be an editor or become a lawyer or think of entering the ministry. None of these professions are easy. You will have to forget the fields of merchandising and shipping, abhor the practice of politics, and forget about the difficult field of medicine. To be a farmer or even a good soldier, you must study and think. My son, you have come into a hard world. I know of only one easy place in it, and that is in the grave."

The leader has the ability to see the big picture. Three men were working on a large building project. One was asked, "What are you doing?" "I'm mixing mortar," he said. The second man said, "I'm helping put up this great stone wall." When the third man was asked, he replied, "I'm building a cathedral to the glory of God." Seeing the big picture and the end result enables the leader to press on with enthusiasm.

One of the major components of genius seems to be hard work. Noah Webster worked 36 years on his Dictionary, while Gibbon laboured 26 years on his "Decline and Fall of the Roman Empire." When Milton was writing "Paradise Lost", he rose at 4:00 a.m. every morning to begin work. Plato wrote the first sentence of the Republic nine different times before it was acceptable to him.

Nothing great was ever achieved without self-discipline.

## THE LEADER STRIVES FOR EXCELLENCE

Going far beyond the call of duty, doing more than others expect ... this is what excellence is all about. It comes from striving, maintaining the highest standards, looking after the smallest detail, and going the extra mile. Excellence means doing your very best in everything you do.

John Gardener, author of "Excellence" said, "The society which scorns excellence in plumbing because plumbing is a humble activity, and tolerates shoddiness in philosophy because it is an exalted activity, will have neither good plumbing nor good philosophy. Neither it's pipes nor it's theories will hold water." [8]

A leader loves excellence and shuns mediocrity. People or companies or nations who do not set high standards will soon be left behind in a world of accelerating change, development, and improvement.

Excellence is not achieved by accident. What we aim at determines what we will become and while we may not always make our goals, our goals will always make us. To aim at excellence is to point your life towards the realization of your potential, to endeavor to fulfill your capabilities.

## DUTY DETERMINES DESTINY.

Great leaders are never satisfied with current levels of performance. They constantly strive for higher and higher levels of achievement.

*"Success has always been easy to measure. It is the distance between one's origins and one's final achievement."*
Michael Korda

Good enough is the enemy of excellence. Effective leaders bring out the best in people by stimulating them to achieve what they thought was impossible.

## EXPECT THE BEST AND YOU WILL GET IT!

As well as expecting the best, people need to be shown that the seemingly impossible performance level is possible.

For years no one believed it possible to run the mile race in under four minutes. Until 1954, the best time was 4:01 by Gunder Haegg in 1945. Conventional wisdom held that the heart just could not stand the added stress of running any faster. Then Roger Bannister proved it could be done with an amazing time of 3:59.4. In a short period of time thereafter twenty six different men broke the four minute mile.

*"The kind of people I look for to fill top management spots are the eager beavers, the mavericks. These are the guys who try to do more than they're expected to do - they always reach."*
Lee Tacocca

The leader should set the example in everything he does. Your team will not respond to requests for better and better results from a leader who does not expect the same from himself or herself.

### IN EXCELLENCE, AS IN EVERY OTHER AREA, YOU CANNOT LEAD FROM BEHIND, YOU MUST LEAD FROM THE FRONT.

Excellence is best described as doing the right things right - selecting the most important things to be done and then accomplishing them one hundred per cent correctly.

Here are some additional tips for securing excellence in your organisation:

1. Make high quality achievement your magnificent obsession. Make quality improvement your number one priority.
2. Recognize those in your team who achieve exceptional quality results.
3. Attack the root causes of poor quality. If you take care in the beginning, the end will take care of itself. (And you will save a great amount of money as well).

Aristotle said, "We are what we repeatedly do". Excellence then, is not an act but a habit. We must resist every situation that allows the good to be the enemy of the best. The wise Solomon stated in Ecclesiastes 9, "Whatever your hand finds to do, do it with all your might."

### SO MANY HAVE GREAT GIFTS, BUT ARE TOO LAZY TO UNWRAP THEM!

Excellence requires quality. It may be quality in management, products, or lifestyle. True success demands quality. The day of junk presentation is over. Study any winner. It is not their cleverness, but the fact that each and every aspect of their business, life or performance is just a touch better than the norm.

No machine or computer can sense quality; only the human being can in product or performance. We must stress excellence over mediocrity. Don't make the mistake of running a business or organization on figures and finances alone or you will go under. Quality is the key to everything we do today.

## THE EXCEPTIONAL LEADER WILL DEMAND QUALITY IN LEADERSHIP, PRODUCTS AND PERFORMANCE.

This philosophy of excellence is discribed in Toyota's "Basic Management Handbook":

"The only acceptable quality percentage is 100%. Every car must be manufactured exactly according to specifications. No Toyota should ever leave the factory without passing quality tests perfectly."

Every business or organization must strive for excellence. It is the responsibility of the leader to ensure it.

*"If there's a way to do it better ... find it."*
Thomas A. Edison

Recess is finally over.

## THE DIFFERENCE BETWEEN GOOD AND GREAT IS A LITTLE EXTRA EFFORT

## HANG TOUGH

It all starts with a dream, which gives a direction to pursue, a goal to achieve. The thing that turns fantasy into reality is the patient discipline of unflagging determination. Leaders do not give up when encountering obstacles or pain. They keep on. When others give up and walk away, they keep on. When others say "It can't be done", they keep on. When laughter and ridicule threaten to turn their dreams to shreds, they keep on. Persistence pays off.

We can dream, think, plan, hope, even pray; but without the grit and discipline of persistence, our lives will be nothing more than empty wishes.

Ask the athlete striving to win gold, or the young woman earning a Ph.D., or the musician perfecting his skill, and each will tell you there is no secret for quick success. The plain truth is that whether we're attempting to master our bodies, a subject, or an instrument, the requirement is the same - a relentless pursuit of the right objectives.

Those with discipline stand the best chance of realizing their fondest dreams.

3. THE
LEADER HAS
WISDOM

—

Wisdom is the
ability to apply
knowledge and
experience to
any given
situation.

**3. THE LEADER HAS WISDOM**

Wisdom is the ability to apply knowledge and experience to any given situation.

"John and Dave were hiking when they spotted a mountain lion staring at them. John froze in his tracks, but Dave sat down on a log, tore off his hiking boots, pulled a pair of running shoes from his backpack and hurriedly began to put them on."

"For crying out loud, you can't outrun a mountain lion!" John screamed.

"I don't have to," shrugged Dave. "I only have to outrun you!" [9]

Well that may be one kind of wisdom! But wisdom is desperately needed by leaders today.

Max Born was one of the great minds of the 20th Century. He was a close friend of Albert Einstein. In an interview on German television before his death, Born commented: "I'd be happier if we had scientists with less brains and more wisdom."

### KNOWLEDGE CAN BE MEMORISED, WISDOM MUST THINK THINGS THROUGH.

Wisdom is the something that enables us to use knowledge rightly. Wisdom resists group pressures, thinks for itself, and is reconciled to the use of its own judgement. It doesn't matter how much money you have; everyone has to buy wisdom on the instalment plan.

Herbert Hoover said, "Wisdom consists not so much in knowing what to do in the ultimate as in knowing what to do next."

## LEADERS GATHER KNOWLEDGE

We are living in an age where knowledge is exploding. Studies have shown that the halfway point of all human knowledge is located less than ten years ago; that is, man's knowledge has doubled within the past decade. Every 60 seconds, 2000 typewritten pages are added to man's knowledge and the material produced every 24 hours takes one person 5 years to read.

If a chemist or physicist sat down and read the scientific journals in their field as their full time job, at the end of a year they would be three months behind in their reading.

More than eighty per cent of all the scientists who have ever lived are alive today. An estimated seventy per cent of the medicines in use today were developed after World War II. Over fifteen thousand scientific journals are being published, many with worldwide circulations.

At the moment we have a computer memory that can assimilate into permanent storage 5 million words per second. That is the same as assimilating the entire Bible 6 times in one second.

The person who thinks he knows everything has a lot to learn!

Thomas A. Edison made the comment, "We do not know one millionth part of one percent about anything. We do not know what water is. We do not know what light is. We do not know what electricity is. We do not know what gravity is. We do not know anything about magnetism. We have a lot of hypotheses, but that is all."

Wisdom is making the best use of knowledge. Develop the ability of discernment. The effective leader has the "insight" needed for any given situation.

Insight is penetration into character or circumstances with understanding. The leader must develop his or her power of insight.

One of the tests of leadership is the ability to recognize a problem before it becomes an emergency.

## LEADERS ARE READERS

The effective leader will develop a regular reading programme. The more knowledge you obtain regarding your particular area of interest, the better you can apply wisdom as it is needed.

Epictetus said, "Only the educated are free". Gaining knowledge will give you the facts you need so that you will not freeze in making decisions. Fear, doubt and worry will immobilize you and prevent you from getting the job done. Reading and studying will help you overcome many of these problems and help you to proceed.

Listen to tapes. Car travel can waste so much valuable time but can be redeemed by listening to good tapes. Top leaders have much of their instruction on video as well. It is time well invested to glean from the advice of others.

Invest time with other leaders as well, not only in your own field, but in other areas as well. Take a leader to lunch. It may cost you a little but the knowledge and wisdom you gain will be well worth the investment. [Remember to keep quiet and let them do the talking!] Have pen and paper handy to record their advice.

Go to conferences or conventions. You need the break and the inspiration.

*"Chance favours the prepared mind."*
Louis Pasteur

A little boy came to his father and asked him, "Dad, who made God?" The father, engrossed in the evening paper responded, "Beats me son." The little boy would not be put off. "Dad, why is the earth round?" The dad answered, "I don't know son." The boy played for a minute then asked, "Dad, is there life on other planets?" The father patiently answered, "Nobody knows the answer to that." Finally the boy asked his father, "Dad, do you mind me asking you all these questions?" The father put down his paper, "Why, not at all son," he said, "how else are you going to learn? "

## TAKE TIME FOR OTHERS

The greatest contribution leaders can make to mankind is to use their power in a positive way - to help and inspire others.

Leaders who accomplish the most will be those who are able to communicate their wisdom effectively to others. They will communicate to subordinates with as much care and attention as they communicate to superiors.

Most members of any group or organization or business want to be "In the know", they want to know what is going on, and how they fit into the picture.

Sharing information about goals and strategies is very important to the success of any organization. People need to know where they are heading before they can make commitments to place group needs above their own. They want frequent, candid information from their immediate boss.

The basic building block of good communication is the feeling that every human being is unique and of value. It has been well said that the finest expression of respect is not praise or status, but a willingness to talk openly to a person. The effective leader will share information openly and willingly. By taking time to share information the leader demonstrates that he or she values the individual as an important member of the organization.

## THE LEADER WHO HAS WISDOM DEMONSTRATES INTEGRITY

More than anything else, followers want to believe that their leaders are ethical and honest. They want to say, "Someday I want to be like him or her."

Corruption and dishonesty seem to occur when the leader loses sight of the fact that he or she is given power for one purpose - to serve others.

## INTEGRITY IS THE MOST IMPORTANT QUALITY IN THE SUCCESS OF THE LEADER.

Dwight D. Eisenhower had these words to say about the importance of integrity:

"In order to be a leader a man must have followers. And to have followers, a man must have their confidence. Hence the supreme quality for the leader is, unquestionably, integrity. Without it no real success is possible no matter whether it is on a section gang, a football field, in the army, or in an office. If a man's associates find him guilty of being phoney, if they find he lacks forthright integrity, he will fail. His teachings and action must square with each other. The first great need, therefore, is integrity and high purpose." [10]

Every time people engage in dishonest or immoral acts, the results come back to haunt them. The key question you must ask yourself is, "What is the right thing to do?"

Here are some suggestions to help maintain your integrity:

1. Be a person who honours your word.
2. Don't lie to cover facts. Nothing increases compatibility like mutual trust and honesty. Credibility is hard to regain.
3. Watch the bribes that may compromise your position.
4. Be responsible for your mistakes and learn from them. Don't "pass the heat on to others" for your mistakes.
5. Guard your tongue. Don't divulge information given in confidence.

People are changed, not by coercion or intimidation, but by example. The example you set, both positive and negative, will establish the standards for your organization.

J. Hanes stated powerfully, "A good name is seldom regained. When character is gone, one of the richest jewels of life is lost forever."

Honesty and integrity are best taught by example.

## A LEADER WITH WISDOM SEEKS GOOD COUNSEL FROM OTHERS

As a President or Prime Minister has their cabinet so, as a leader you must cultivate a group of tried and trusted people that can advise you and supplement your wisdom and knowledge. Learn to accept good advice.

What qualities would you look for in people who could advise you? Here are some:

1. Someone who has your best interests at heart. They will stay with you even through the tough times.
2. Someone who is consistent. They must have the points on the board.
3. Someone who will be straight with you. You don't want a "yes" man, or someone who will just pat you on the back all the time.
4. Someone who is positive, not negative. You can't afford the luxury of negativity or you will end up with bad advice.
5. Someone who accepts you warts and all.
6. Someone who is filled with common sense.
7. Someone who is the soul of discretion. You need someone you can trust to keep confidences.

A good advisor will prove to be more precious than gold to you and will help so much with wise counsel.

### BE A LEADER WHO EXERCISES WISDOM.

**4. THE LEADER HAS COURAGE**

—

Courage is
not the
absence of
fear; it is the
mastery of it.

**4. THE LEADER HAS COURAGE**

Courage is not the absence of fear; it is the mastery of it.

Success is never final, and failure is never fatal; it is courage that counts.

COURAGE. It has several names: bravery, valour, fearlessness, audacity, chivalry, heroism, confidence, nerve... and a few nicknames; guts, grit, gristle, backbone, pluck, and spunk. But whatever the name, it's never met its match. The heights of the Himalayas only encourage it. The depths of the Caribbean merely excite it. The sounds of war stimulate it. The difficulty of a job motivates it. The demands of competition inspire it. Criticism challenges it...adventure arouses it...danger incites it...threats quicken it.

COURAGE. That's another word for inner strength, presence of mind against odds, determination to hang in there, to venture, persevere, and withstand hardship. It's got "keeping" power. It's what kept the pioneers rolling forward in those covered wagons in spite of the elements and mountains and flaming arrows. It's what makes the amputee reject pity and continue to take life by the throat. It's what forces every married couple having trouble, never to say, "Let's terminate". It's what encourages the divorcee to face tomorrow. It's what keeps a nation free in spite of attacks.

Are you ready to run when the heat rises? About to quit? Every day, in some way, your courage will be tested.

Courage is a three letter word. Real courage is saying "yes" to life, not backing down when we face adversity. Courage is acting with fear, not without it.

*"Courage is doing what you're afraid to do. There can be no courage when you're scared."*
Eddie Rickenbacker

*"Success is never final, and failure is never fatal; it's courage that counts."*
Unknown

"The Pilgrims displayed dramatic courage. On December 21 1620 the voyaging Mayflower dropped anchor in Plymouth Bay with Captain Christopher Jones at her helm. It had been a gruelling voyage, taking the one hundred and twenty ton capacity ship sixty-six days to make the perilous crossing. There had been disease, anxiety, and childbirth among the 102 courageous passengers. Furthermore, they arrived on the black New England shore during a hard winter which ultimately claimed half of their number. However, when spring came and the captain of the Mayflower offered free passage to anyone desiring to return, not a single person accepted.

These chivalrous souls had dedicated themselves to the total cause of freedom. They had come to a wilderness to carve out a better way of life. Faith prompted the voyage; faith sustained the Pilgrims and their religious convictions constrained them to raise their voices in praise. Their hardship, sacrifice, devotion, concept of government, and vigorous religion all remind us of those who sought a country." [11]

## LEADERS LEAD FROM THE FRONT, NOT FROM THE REAR

Leadership is often a battle, and the fight requires courage. Having courage doesn't mean you'll have no inner turmoil. Having courage means that you will do what is right, regardless of the consequences. One leader said, "Leaders choose their battles. They can't win every one. They may even lose a few along the way. But they can win the war."

*"Courage is resistance to fear, mastery of fear - not absence of fear."*
Mark Twain

I will never forget seeing a painting of Viscount Nelson, Great Britian's greatest admiral and naval hero. He defeated the combined French and Spanish fleets at Trafalgar in the greatest naval victory in British history. His victory broke the naval power of France, and established Great Britian's rule of the seas for the rest of the 1800's.

Nelson chased the French to the West Indies and back. It was more than two years before he was able to bring the French to battle off Cape Trafalgar on the coast of Spain, on 21st October 1805. Nelson hoisted his famous signal, "England expects that every man will do his duty." With only 27 vessels he attacked the combined French and Spanish fleets. One of the great naval battles of all time followed. Napoleon's fleet, with a total of thirty-three warships, was destroyed. [12]

In the painting, at the height of the battle, stood Nelson. One of his arms hung lifeless at his side, mangled and amputated in a previous battle. He only had the sight of one eye; again the result of another battle. Here stood this one-eyed, one-armed, battered, naval hero. His officers pleaded with him to disguise himself and not stand boldly on the deck in his bright red uniform. The snipers' bullets were whistling through the air. Cannon balls were ripping the rigging and sails. He was a fighter. He said, "I am of the opinion that the boldest measures are the safest." With so many odds against them he knew he had to impart courage to his men. Without flinching, he stood, studying the battle, commanding the fleet.

Nelson was wounded at the height of the battle. He was carried below with a sharpshooter's bullet in his spine. He died during the battle, but he lived long enough to know that the British fleet had defeated the French and Spanish fleets. Nelson's last words were, "Thank God I have done my duty." He had the ability to inspire men with his own courage and confidence. His frail body housed a great spirit.

*"One man with courage is a majority."*
Andrew Jackson

There are those that you lead that need the encouragement of your courage. As a leader you need to conquer and kill anything that robs you of courage.

What are some of the things that kill courage?

## DESTROY DISTRACTING WORRY

Worry has been termed, the "official emotion of our age", and "one of the most urgent problems of our day". It has well been described as the world's greatest modern plague. Worry is an enemy waiting to destroy us. Real or imaginary, worry saps our strength, fills us with tension, affects our health and well-being, and robs us of joy and peace of mind. The exciting news is that it can be conquered.

Worry has a way of commanding our total attention. Instead of keeping on target, we zig-zag through life, our thoughts always returning to our real or imagined worries.

Don't allow yourself to get sidetracked through worry. Worry will rob you of precious time and energy. Worry will hinder you from achieving your goals by clouding your vision.

Worry causes confusion and fear. As you set goals for your life they eliminate confusion and fear.

Keep on target. One of the most effective ways to overcome worry is to set goals, both short-term and long-term. You may be a homemaker. Set a goal to finish your housekeeping in, say, two hours rather than dwelling on your cares and problems. You may be concerned as a businessman that your income is dropping. Instead of wasting precious time and energy, set a plan of attack.

You can slice your cares in half by asking the following questions:

1. What is the real problem?
2. What is the cause of the problem?
3. What are the possible solutions to the problem?
4. What solution is best?

## WORRY IS THE ADVANCE INTEREST YOU PAY ON TROUBLES THAT NEVER COME.

A businessman drew up what he called a "Worry Chart" in which he kept a record of his worries. He discovered that forty percent of them were about things that probably would never happen; thirty percent concerned past decisions that he could not now unmake; twelve percent dealt with other people's criticism of him, and ten percent were worries about his health. He concluded that only eight percent of them were really legitimate.

There are two days in every week about which we should be kept free from fear and apprehension.

One of these days is yesterday, with its mistakes and cares, its aches and pains, its faults and blunders. Yesterday has passed beyond our control. All the money in the world cannot bring back yesterday. We cannot erase a single word we have spoken.

The other day we should not worry about is tomorrow with its possible adversities, its burdens, and its great promise. Tomorrow also is beyond our immediate control, it is yet unborn.

That leaves one day only - today. You can fight the battles of just one day. It is only when we add the burdens of yesterday and tomorrow that we are likely to break under the load.

There is a great difference between worry and concern. A worried person sees the problem; the concerned person solves the problem. It's not that you go through life seemingly as a great big giggle and laugh. No, you simply refuse to allow negative worry habits to dominate and control you, which would make it impossible for you to function effectively.

It has been medically proven that worry causes sickness. People say, "I'm sick from worry." A study was made of one hundred executives of the average age of forty-four years and it was discovered that half of them had high blood pressure, heart disease, or ulcers. It was notable in every case that worry was a prominent factor. It is a simple fact of life that our bodies function well when our minds are free from worry, anxiety, stress, fear and tension.

Worry is like a rocking chair - it will give you something to do but it won't get you anywhere.

Worry is the misuse of the imagination.

## LEARN TO CONTROL FEAR

One of the main reasons people fail in their job or career is because of fear. Fear paralyses people.

## THE FEAR OF FAILURE

Leaders are people who are not afraid to fail. They have the ability to accept their failures and continue on, knowing that failure is a natural consequence of trying. The law of failure is one of the most powerful of all the success laws because you only really fail when you quit trying.

*"Failure is only the opportunity to move intelligently and begin again."*
Henry Ford

*"The greatest mistake a man can make is to be afraid of making one."*
Elbert Hubbard

Remember you never fail if you are doing your best. You can turn a failure into a success if you learn from it. You grow by your failings.

Attitudes are a secret power working 24 hours a day, for good or bad.

*"Remember you will not always win. Some days, the most resourceful individual will taste defeat. But there is in this case always tomorrow - after you have done your best to achieve success today."*
Maxwell Maltz

Most successful leaders fail time and time again. It's not whether or not you fail but whether you have the courage to get up again.

A positive attitude is a person's passport to a better tomorrow. A misty morning does not signify a cloudy day.

## THE FEAR OF SUCCESS

Some are afraid to launch out into the deep for fear they might be successful. They are not sure they can handle it and so prefer to stay in the comfort zone.

You will never gain the sight of some distant harbour if you are afraid of losing sight of the shore.

What does fear and anxiety do? It doesn't empty tomorrow of its problems, but it empties today of its strength. It doesn't make you escape trouble, but it makes you unfit to handle it when it comes.

Here are some of the most common forms of fear:
The fear of poverty
The fear of criticism
The fear of ill health
The fear of the loss of the love of someone
The fear of old age
The fear of death
The fear of failure
The fear of heights
The fear of disease
The fear of crowds
The fear of rejection
The fear of unemployment
The fear of what others say about you
The fear of moving away
The fear of being yourself
The fear of buying or selling
The fear of the loss of finance
The fear of war
The fear of the dark
The fear of being alone
to name a few!

The misfortunes hardest to bear are those which rarely happen.

Fear causes us to worry and threatens to destroy our inner peace and outward poise. It uses scare tactics and surprise attacks. It waits to attack you at your most vulnerable moment. No poison so effectively robs the mind of all its powers of action and reason than fear.

An old Indian fable tells of a mouse which was in constant distress because of its fear of the rat. A magician took pity on it and turned it into a cat. Immediately it became afraid of the dog. So the magician turned it into a tiger. Immediately it began to fear the hunter. Then the magician said: "Be a mouse again. You have only the heart of a mouse and I cannot help you."

All forms of fear produce fatigue. No wonder so many are drained of vim and vitality. Fear drains energy. One of the greatest keys to leadership is energy. Study any leader and you will discover one of their great secrets is their tireless energy.

Florence Nightingale would work twenty four hours at a stretch.

John Wesley travelled on horseback the equivalent of ten times around the earth's equator.

Fear will cut a channel into which all other thoughts drain. You cannot afford the luxury of allowing worry to deplete your energy.

Fear stops you from trying. Your fears will stop you unless you stop them first.

The positive mind has extra problem solving power.

## CREATE YOUR OWN COURAGE

He was a man in his twenties. During those years he drifted. When he turned thirty-one, he thought, "I've got to get myself going and do something". He formed a partnership and went into business. In one and a half years he lost everything and went bankrupt. Then he decided that since he was broke anyway, he should go into politics. In his first local election, he lost badly. Two years later, when he was thirty-four, he decided to go back into business. He went bankrupt again. A year later he thought things were getting better, and he fell in love with a beautiful woman. She died. So the next year, at age thirty-six, he had a nervous breakdown and was confined to his bed for months.

He finally shook that off, and two years later he decided to run for another local election. He lost. He went into another business, and he made a little bit of money. Then at forty-three, he ran for Congress. He lost. At forty-six, he ran for Congress again. He lost again. At forty-eight he ran for the Senate. He lost that election as well. When he was fifty-five years of age, he tried for the nomination of his party for Vice-President, and was defeated badly. At age fifty-eight, he ran for the Senate again. Once again he lost. Finally, at sixty years of age, Abraham Lincoln was elected to his first office - President of the United States. Do you know that Lincoln said to friends late in life that he had had a lifelong battle with fear and depression, but he wouldn't quit?

Lincoln was a fighter, a man of courage, a winner. He overcame countless private fears and endless public rejections to attain the highest job in the country.

*"You gain strength, courage and confidence by every experience, but you must stop, and look fear in the face... You must do the thing you think you cannot do."*
Eleanor Roosevelt

Here are some suggestions to create courage:

1. Live for a great and a high cause. What great dreams do you have that keep you awake at night?
2. Remember, people are counting on you. Your family, your organization, your team.
3. Keep your dreams vividly before you at all times. Obstacles are what you see when you take your eyes off the goals.

Remember - Courage is not the absence of fear but the mastery of it.

## 5. THE LEADER HAS HUMILITY

—

One of the
surest
evidences of
greatness is
a humble
spirit.

**5. THE LEADER HAS HUMILITY**

*"If I could see further than others, it was because I stood on the shoulders of giants."*
Isaac Newton

Mention was made earlier of Great Britain's greatest admiral and naval hero, Viscount Horatio Nelson. One of Nelson's great characteristics as a commander was his willingness to give full credit to his officers and men. After the Battle of Copenhagen, he refused an honour given to him by the City of London, because he alone was to be honoured. Nelson replied, "Never till the City of London thinks justly of the merits of my brave companions on 2 April can I, their commander, receive any attention from the City of London."

The poet Robert Southey wrote of Nelson, "England has had many heroes. But never one who so entirely possessed the love of his fellow countrymen. All men knew that his heart, was as humane as it was fearless... that with perfect and entire devotion he served his country with all his heart, and with all his soul, and with all his strength. And therefore they loved him as truly and fervently as he loved England." [13]

Humility is such an important characteristic in the life of the leader. Most people cannot stand folk who are full of themselves no matter what their successes are. However, true humility is appreciated by all.

Toscanini was so humble that when his orchestra burst into applause at a rehearsal because they realized the heights to which he had lifted them, he said with tears in his eyes, "It is not me, it is Beethoven."

A friend once asked the famous conductor of a great symphony orchestra which instrument in the orchestra he considered was the most difficult to play? Without hesitation the leader answered, "The second fiddle. I can get plenty of first violinists. But to find one who can play second fiddle with enthusiasm - that's the problem. And if we have no second fiddle, we have no harmony."

So much of life's frustration, pain and unhappiness comes because we make ourselves the centre of our lives. We insist on living motivated by a self-regard that throws life out of focus.

Living for self never satisfies. Have you noticed the letter "I" is in the middle of pride, sin and anxiety?

One of the surest evidences of greatness is a humble spirit. The first test of a truly great person is their humility. A humble person can neither be put down nor exalted; they can neither be humiliated nor honoured; they remain the same person under all circumstances.

Queen Mary, in her time, visited a hospital ward one day and paused at the bedside of a little girl. She asked the child where she lived and the child said in Battersea, a poor district in London.

"Where do you live?" the girl asked, unaware of the rank of her visitor.

"Oh, just behind Gorringe's department store", Queen Mary replied.

## LEADERS WHO ARE SECURE HAVE NOTHING TO PROTECT

Leadership requires that men and women recognize what they have to do and work towards doing it. They do not keep on expecting recognition for every achievement.

True leadership happens when people want to see the work done and they care little about who gets the credit.

There are those who feign humility because they want more praise for their accomplishments, which gives them greater assurances of their worth.

Real leaders see themselves as a team. Their fragile ego does not have to be propped up by rewards. However, as the rewards come they want to share the limelight with others.

Will Rogers used to say, "Get someone else to blow your horn, and the sound will carry twice as far!"

From an experience of her childhood, Mrs Floyd Crook recalls how a great truth was impressed upon her with special meaning. She writes, "I came home from school one day crying because I had been given only a small part in the children's programme, while my playmate got the leading role. After drying my tears, my mother took off her watch and put it in my hand. "What do you see?" she asked. "A gold case, a face, and two hands," I replied. Opening the back, she repeated the same question. I told her I saw many tiny wheels. "This watch would be useless," she said, "without every part - even the ones you can hardly see." "The object lesson has helped me all through life to see the importance of the small duties we're asked to perform."[14]

Samuel Chadwick, the great preacher wisely said, "If you're successful, don't crow. If you fail, don't croak." Peter Marshall, another well known preacher prayed, "Lord, when we are wrong, make us willing to change. And when we are right, make us easy to live with."

"A good leader," said Arnold Glasow, "takes a little more than his share of the blame, and a little less than his share of the credit."

William Carey, sometimes called "the father of modern missions", always seemed to have a humble spirit. In young manhood he had a job repairing shoes. As the years went by, honours were heaped upon him because of his many accomplishments. Yet this unassuming man would only accept positions and appointments that opened the way to more work in Christ's service. Even at the zenith of his popularity, one of his most striking characteristics was his meek and selfless attitude. A state dinner was given in his honour. With a sneer, a jealous English officer asked the host, "Wasn't your great Dr Carey once just a shoemaker?" Before the man could reply, the renowned missionary, who was near enough to hear the remark, answered with quiet dignity, "No sir, I was not that skilled. I was only a cobbler." [15]

DON'T LET SUCCESS GO TO YOUR HEAD.
REMEMBER - WHEN SUCCESS COMES YOUR
WAY, WALK IN HUMILITY.

A mother whale once warned her son, "Remember, it's when you go to the top and start blowing that you get harpooned!"

Leaders, because of their natures, tend to have blind spots. You may need a trusted friend to tell you how you are coming across to people. We are in a constant state of change. The leader needs constant appraisal. No one has arrived. No one has got it completely together.

## THE EFFECTIVE LEADER IS TEAM-CENTRED

The great paradox of life is that the more you give of yourself, the more you receive. You need to build a reservoir of good will by placing the interests of other people above your own.

You need to be sensitive to the needs and feelings of your team or organisation. You need to support them, help them, and be concerned for their well-being. The true leader will subordinate his or her own needs to those of others.

Morale and productivity are highest in groups when leaders show a high degree of consideration and concern for their team. Most people appreciate a leader who takes a sincere interest in them.

Each human being has the right to be treated with dignity. We accomplish success through other people. Nothing can be accomplished without the involvement of other individuals.

Fair, firm and friendly is the secret. Treating others as you would like to be treated. Play no favourites. Getting a fair deal is the most important concern to employees at all levels.

The effective leader has the ability to make others feel good about themselves. Giving consideration, demonstrating concern and being fair creates a strong bond between the leader and his or her team.

## THE EFFECTIVE LEADER IS A GOOD LISTENER

To make people feel important, you must listen carefully to them. Listening attentively is one of the best ways to show respect for anyone on your team. It demonstrates that you believe the individual has worthwhile thoughts and is a valuable member of your organisation or group. When people feel needed, they tend to take more interest in what they do.

Careful listening shows that a leader has humility. It demonstrates that he is not too aloof or too busy or too self-opinionated to spend time listening to another idea or opinion.

Problems can often be resolved before they have time to escalate. Don't rely on others in your organization to inform you how things are going, find out first-hand yourself. The leader is vulnerable to the sudden surfacing of morale problems if he or she is not in tune with what is going on. Listening to others on a first-hand level will enable you to take corrective action early.

The most important good listening habit is to totally concentrate on what the person is saying.

Leaders who make it a practice to draw out the thoughts and ideas of their team and who are receptive even to bad news will be properly informed.

Here are some ways to be a better listener:

1. Ask questions
2. Give undivided attention
3. Maintain eye contact
4. Take notes
5. Take the phone off the hook.
6. Don't just listen to words, study body language, facial expressions and tone of voice.
7. Wait until you clearly understand what a person is saying before you give a reply.
8. Do not jump to conclusions.
9. Listen to everyone, not just to those you like or respect.
10. Allow them time to fully express themselves even if you do not agree with them. Let them get it off their chests.
11. Make it easy for people to see you.

Remember that when your team no longer believes their leader listens to them, they start looking around for someone who will.

## THE LEADER KNOWS HOW TO ENJOY LIFE AND LAUGH

### TAKE TIME TO LAUGH.
### IT IS THE MUSIC OF THE SOUL.

It was with insight that Ethel Barrymore said, "You grow up the day you have the first real laugh - at yourself. And Sydney Harris said, "God cannot be solemn, or He would not have blessed man with the incalculable gift of laughter."

The great leader Sir Winston Churchill said, "It is my belief you cannot deal with the most serious things in the world unless you understand the most amusing."

The leader needs to learn to laugh to help defuse the tension he or she so often is under. To make someone laugh or help them enjoy life is one of the most precious gifts available today.

It takes 72 muscles to frown and only 14 to smile so it's more economical anyway.

Charles H. Spurgeon, the London preacher, was emphasizing to his class the importance of making your facial expression harmonize with your speech. "When you speak of Heaven," he said, "let your face light up, let it be irradiated with a heavenly gleam, let your eyes shine with reflected glory. But when you speak of Hell - well, then your ordinary face will do!"

If only happiness were as contagious as the common cold. Don't keep looking for happiness, give it and it will come back to you. Happiness is not the station you arrive at but the way you travel. King George V of England would say, "The secret of happiness is not doing what one likes, but in liking what one has to do."

Scientists have been studying the effects of laughter on human beings and have found, among other things, that laughter has a profound and instantaneous effect on virtually every important organ in the human body. Laughter reduces health-sapping tensions and relaxes the tissues as well as exercising the most vital organs. It is said that laughter, even when forced, results in beneficial effects on us, both mentally and physically. So next time you feel nervous and jittery, indulge in a good laugh. [16]

Here are some practical points to help find and maintain real joy and happiness:

1. Count your blessings. There are millions who would trade places with you right now.
2. It is not what we have, but who we are. Learn to live in the now. Not tomorrow, or next week, or next month, or next year, not in the future, but "NOW".

3. The great key to real joy is in serving others. People are bad spellers; they spell service - "serve-us".
4. Joy and happiness are a choice. There is only one good thing about misery - it's optional!
5. Real joy and happiness is found in God alone. We need to get back to the Maker's instructions.

Remember, it takes 72 muscles to frown - and only 14 to smile.

**6. THE LEADER IS A DECISION MAKER**

—

You are a
product of
your own
choice

**6. THE LEADER IS A DECISION MAKER**

You are a product of your choices.

You will become the sum of the little choices in life. Not to decide is to decide not to. The leader lives life on the attack.

As a house is built brick by brick, so our lives are built decision by decision. Each one of these decisions compose a collective destiny.

Successful people tend to make decisions quickly and change them rarely, while unsuccessful people tend to make decisions slowly and change them often. Indecision is often lack of energy. You have the power and the privilege of choice.

There are three times when it is not good to make an important decision:

1. When you are sick.
2. When you are tired.
3. When you are travelling.

## ORGANIZE THE DECISION-MAKING PROCESS

Effective leaders constantly work at making decisions simple.

A good leader knows that there are certain rules to follow to make the right decisions. Here are some guidelines:

1. Clarify the issue. What is the decision that I am trying to make? Boil the issue down to it's simplest form.

2. Gather the facts. The most frequent mistake made in decision-making is trying to decide before all the facts are known. While I have said that good leaders make decisions quickly that does not negate the importance of gathering as many relevent, proven facts. Don't rely on assumptions, get the facts.

Refuse to be pressured into a decision. Often your team will want direction "now". Let's get it settled now. Often we are compelled to make decisions too quickly. Base your decision on facts, not assumptions. You are not looking for the handiest alternative but you must come to grips with the real issues involved. Don't try to escape the issue with snap decisions. You may have to do the hard work of brainstrain but it is worth it in the long haul.

It has been well said that once the facts are clear, the decisions jump out at you.

3. What risk does it involve? This is when you ask two questions:
    a. What's the worst thing that could happen? This is when the pessimists come to life.
    b. What's the best thing that could happen? This is when all your optimists spring into action!

Then ask the question, "Is it worth the risk?"

Try and get your team to agree on the risk being taken so that at some later date, if there is disagreement, it was recorded that you all agreed on the decision.

All decision making has an element of risk, but that does not mean that we take foolish risks.

4. Get good counsel. You may need legal advice, or financial advice. (If you are after financial advice, try and find out how much he has in the bank!) Find out who has good expertise in that area. Even if you have to pay a little, it may save you a lot.
5. How will this decision affect those involved? Consideration should be given to your team, others involved, spouses, and children.
6. Try to determine the results of the decision in the future. Think down the road five, ten years or more from now.
7. Honestly answer the questions:

a. Is it illegal?
b. Is it immoral?
c. Is it unethical?
8. Is my heart at peace? Try and make sure all your questions are answered to your satisfaction.

A leader is a person of action and to be a person of action you must master the art of decision-making. Grow in maturity in leadership by being responsibly decisive.

Successful leaders have the courage to take action where others hesitate. Your decisions will always be better if you do what is right for the organisation or group, not what is right for yourself.

You don't have to come up with all the answers, all the time, but you have to be prepared to endorse them where necessary. Once a decision is made then move forward. Look for the next challenge.

As much as possible, keep your team involved in the decision-making process. Ask for ideas, input, thoughts before important actions are taken. People carry out decisions that they have participated in making much more enthusiastically. Involvement leads to commitment.

In the final analysis, the decision-making burden belongs to the leader. You cannot please everyone with your decisions, nor should you try.

If it is possible try and make the decision on the spot or at least set a final date for doing so.

## WHAT IF THE LEADER MAKES A WRONG DECISION?

Every effective leader will make a wrong decision at some time or other, what counts however, is how you handle it. Willingly admit it. Don't try to cover up. Your team know that you are not infallible! As you take corrective action you will usually be forgiven by the group. I don't think that I have ever made a small mistake in my life! As long as people see that you are trying to do what is best for the organisation they will stand with you.

## THE LEADER HAS A STRONG SENSE OF URGENCY

It was Goethe who said, "The right man is the one who seizes the moment." And Will Rogers came up with the brilliant statement, "Even though you're on the right track - you'll get run over if you just sit there."

**WITH REPEATED SUCCESS PEOPLE TEND TO GET COMPLACENT.**

It is important to maintain a feeling of excitment. That's why it is important to keep taking on new challenges. If the captain relaxes too long, the crew will go on vacation. As a leader, you must maintain your own sense of urgency.

*"No one keeps up his enthusiasm automatically. Enthusiasm must be nourished with new actions, new aspirations, new efforts, new vision. It is one's own fault if one's enthusiasm is gone; you have failed to feed it."*
[Papyrus]

If there is one thing that a leader should fear, it is complacency. You, or your organization should never lose the will to win. As a leader you must set the example of urgency for others to follow.

One of the tests of leadership is the ability to recognize a problem before it becomes an emergency, and act immediately.

## THE LEADER AND TIME MANAGEMENT

You only have one life, one shot at it, so make it count.

Time is your most valuable personal resource. Use it wisely because it can't be replaced.

Time management skills can be developed and perfected and will lead you on to greater productivity and performance.

Here are a few well known tips for daily time planning:

1. Create a daily - "To do" list. (It is best to write it out the night before).
2. List goals and set priorities. A.B.C.
3. Do A's first.
4. Handle each piece of paper once only.
5. Do it now!
6. Right now, what is the best use of my time?

Disciplined focus is what distinguishes those who make things happen from those who watch things happen.

Here are some of the techniques used by successful leaders to make the best use of their most precious commodity - time.

1. Do the most important things first. Sometimes we avoid difficult or disagreeable tasks. Force yourself to do these tasks first then reward youself. Don't waste time on unimportant things. Very little can stand against sustained, single-minded, pursuit of your goals.

2. Don't try to do everything at once. Focus only on the areas that will benefit most from your leadership expertise. Concentrate on a few things at a time. Stick to them until you are satisfied they are under control.

3. Limit interruptions as much as possible. Guard your best working times. If necessary, work on a problem in a secluded area. Interruptions are the number one time wasters.

4. Handle your mail promptly. Unattended mail causes stress. Set time aside when you will open and attend to your mail. Procrastination results in mail accumulating, requiring action. Throw away unnecessary mail, give it to your secretary, or send it to the required department for their action.

5. Set deadlines. This will force you to accomplish projects quickly.

6. Think - how can I do it better? Set quality time aside to think about creative ways to improve the performance of your organization. Peak performance comes through pondering. This may well prove to be invaluable to you. When you are relaxed, brainstorm your situation. You will be amazed at the ideas that spring to light. The leader, as well as having vision, must inspire others.

7. You don't have to attend every meeting. Be very selective regarding meetings. Probably about half of them we don't need to attend. Maybe someone else can go in your place and give you a report. Whatever meetings you do attend, encourage brevity.

8. Control visitors. There is often a fine line in sharing time and wasting time. "Can I have a moment of your time?", is the opening line that can interrupt valuable time. You want to keep the lines of communication open but not waste time.

It may be possible to have a "holding station", a lounge or area that is not in your office. Once people are in your office it is hard to get them to leave. You may find it helpful to remain standing if it is just small talk. People get down to business faster when they are on their feet. Perhaps you can organize a more suitable time to meet them later. It is very important that you don't appear impolite.

9. Invest your time where it pays the most. Often we invest huge amounts of time where there is little return for the effort. You may have to spend time doing some honest thinking to analyse

your time investments. Do not waste your high energy hours. Invest them where they produce the highest payoff.

10. Delegate responsibility. As Moses' father-in-law encouraged him to delegate the leadership responsibilities to others, so must the leader make the most use of his or her time by sharing the workload. Then you must allow your team to put their personal stamp on projects assigned to them. Like Lazarus, "loose them and let them go". Try and set completion times for accomplishment.

11. Don't allow worry to distract you. Worry is like a rocking chair, it will give you something to do but it won't get you anywhere! You can slice your worries in half by asking the following questions:

[1] What is the real problem?
[2] What is the cause of the problem?
[3] What are all the possible solutions to the problem?
[4] What solution is the best?

12. Keep your mind on the project in hand. Too often, as we work on a particular project, our minds drift off on to some other thing we know that needs doing. "A double-minded man is unstable in all his ways." [James 1:8] It is important to discipline our minds to keep on with what we are doing at that moment.

13. Keep paper and pen handy to record inspirational thoughts. You may wake during the night with a great idea. Write it down straight away. A thought may come to you as you work on another project. Write it down straight away. This will help you to keep your mind on the subject and also that precious thought will not escape. The old saying is true that a blunt pencil will always remember more than a sharp mind.

14. Use travel time. Waiting for a plane, driving, picking up your children, can all be used to redeem time by reading, listening to a tape or having someone with you to invest time into their life. The most successful leaders never waste a moment.

15. Spend time relaxing. Holidays or days off are not wasted time. They are called recreation. And you do need to be re-created to be an effective leader.

16. Use the telephone correctly. Write down a quick agenda before you use the phone (especially if it is long distance). Remember, the telephone is your servant. Sometimes you may have to ignore it completely or take it off the hook. Maybe your secretary or spouse can screen the calls for you. Train your team to use a fax machine. That way you have an accurate record.

## THE ADVANTAGES OF TIME MANAGEMENT

When you control your time you accomplish important goals, and free up your nights and weekends for other family activities. Controlling your time helps overcome frustration and brings your life into balance and order giving you the feeling of control and poise. Better planning of your time enables you to give yourself more to others. You feel better on top of the pile than under it. Life will take on a greater zest, enthusiasm and productivity. You will be able to handle a crisis far more easily and it will give you more time for planning.

Develop yourself as a decisive leader.

**7. THE LEADER DEVELOPS FRIENDSHIPS**

—

We all need
someone
we can be
open with.
No one
makes it
alone.

**7. THE LEADER DEVELOPS FRIENDSHIPS**

Success in life depends upon the support and help of other people. No one makes it alone.

Henry Ford used to say, "My best friend is the one that brings out the best in me."

Work hard at building successful relationships. Without friendship one is doomed to loneliness. Value your friendships. Tell your friends you appreciate them. A friend is an island of safety where you feel secure and where communication is often without sound.

Work on relationships constantly. Don't take a friend for granted. Unless it is kept constantly polished up then a relationship can get a little dusty or rusted. Use the phone, a letter or a visit, a card or a gift.

A successful relationship is based on mutual respect. Recognise your own self-worth and the self-worth of others.

One of the great problems we face today in modern society is the scarcity of good friends. It takes a lot of forgiving to be a friend. Friendship is the art of overlooking the failings of others. A friend is one who puts his finger on a fault without rubbing it in! The old Chinese proverb says, "Do not use a hatchet to remove a fly from your friend's forehead".

It was George Elliot who said, "Friendship is the inexpressible comfort of feeling safe with a person, having neither to weigh thoughts nor measure words."

To gain friends, become interested in other people instead of trying to get them interested in you. Friendship is not only doing something for someone, it is caring for someone, which is what every person needs.

Talk with a close friend about your cares and worries. It will help so much. A problem shared is a problem halved. An old Swedish proverb says, "Shared joy is a double joy. Shared sorrow is half a sorrow".

Maturity is that stage in life where you don't have to see eye to eye with a person but you can walk arm in arm. It is possible to disagree and still be agreeable.

We all need someone we can be open with. They will know our secrets - our hiding places, our soft spots - our hopes and dreams. This is what real friendship is all about.

After a visit to the palace to see Queen Victoria, the great poet Alfred Lord Tennyson commented, "Up there, in all her glory and splendour, she was lonely." Nothing, whether it is royal status, wealth, public success, or bustling activism, can remove that need we have for other people. "People who need people are the luckiest people in the world," says the old song. The truth is, they are the only people in the world. When God created man He said, "It is not good for man to be alone" [Genesis 2:8]. He made us for relationships, for friendships, for companionship.

There was an old spinster at one time who was sharing her plight with the Pastor. "Well," said the Pastor, "God made man and God made woman and you can't improve on that." "I don't want to improve on it," she wailed. "I just want to get in on it!"

The first attempt of David Livingstone to preach ended in failure. "Friends, I have forgotten all I have to say," he gasped, and in shame stepped from the pulpit! At that moment Robert Moffat, who was visiting Edinburgh, advised David not to give up. Perhaps he could be a doctor instead of a preacher, he advised. Livingstone decided to be both. When the years of medical study were done, he went to Africa. Moffat proved to be a true friend.

I went out to find a friend,
But could not find one there,
I went out to be a friend,
And friends were everywhere!

*"The world is so empty if one thinks only of mountains, rivers,
and cities; but to know someone who thinks and feels with me,
and who, though distant, is close to me in spirit, this makes the
earth for me an inhabited garden."*
[The German Poet - "Goethe"]

The only way to have a friend is to be one. Choose your friends for
what they are, and not what they have or have to be. Promises may
get friends but it is performances that keep them. Few men have
the natural strength to honour a friend's success without envy.

*"Associate yourself with men of good quality if you esteem your
own reputation; for 'tis better to be alone than in bad company."*
George Washington

A real friend is one who will talk to you on the phone even though
he knows he is missing his favourite television programme!

When we lose a friend we die a little. An old Russian proverb says,
"An old friend is better than two new ones". If you really want to
know who your friends are, just make a mistake! When problems
come knocking at your door you don't have to answer it alone
when you are blessed with true friends. The person that ceases to
be your friend never was a good one.

## MAKE YOUR SPOUSE YOUR BEST FRIEND

The greatest asset you have in life, if you are married, is your
spouse. Never take the relationship for granted. Be creative. Plan
various ways to date your mate. Do things together. Walk together,
talk together. Share presents and gifts. The stronger your

relationship, the stronger and more effective you will be as a leader.

Keep the candle of romance burning brightly in your marriage by:

Giving your smile to your partner - freely, regularly and lovingly.

Giving words of praise. Appreciate your partner for his or her efforts, commitments, love or hard work.

Giving words of encouragement in the areas which your mate may be finding difficult or even monotonous.

Giving a small love note or card.

Giving comfort when your loved one needs your arms to reassure him or her.

Giving a small gift regularly - just to keep the message coming through loudly and clearly - "You're special".

Giving your energy to the tasks which will lighten your partner's work load a little.

Giving and affirming your love verbally and by tender touch. Keep on saying to each other, "I love you".

## HOW TO MAKE FRIENDS

1. Be likeable. Practise being the kind of person people like.

2. Take the initiative. Risk making the first move. Introduce yourself as opportunities come.

3. Get the other person's name right and make sure they get your name right. A person's name is the sweetest word in the English

language. (Or any other for that matter!) Greet people by name. Look people in the eye.

4. Don't expect anyone to be perfect. Accept human differences and limitations.

   A friend is one who knows you as you are, understands where you have been, accepts who you have become and still gently invites you to grow.

5. Find qualities to admire in a person. G.K. Chesterton used to say, "The truly great person is the one who makes every person feel great."

6. Practise conversation. Encourage others to talk. In Queen Victoria's time, a young woman had the good fortune to be escorted to dinner by William E. Gladstone, who was considered one of the most brilliant statesmen of the 19th Century. On the following evening, the same young lady was escorted by Benjamin Disraeli, novelist, statesman and twice prime minister of Great Britian.

   When asked for her impression of these two great rivals, she replied, "After an evening with Gladstone, I thought he was the most brilliant man I have ever met. After an evening with Disraeli, I thought myself to be the most fascinating woman in the world!" [17]

7. Practise being courteous at all times.

*"A blessed thing it is for any man or woman to have a friend: one human soul whom we can trust utterly; who knows the best and the worst of us, and who loves us, in spite of all our faults; who will speak the honest truth to us, while the world flatters us to our face, and laughs at us behind our back; who will give us counsel and reproof in the day of prosperity and self-conceit; but*

*who will cheer us in the day of difficulty and sorrow, when the world leaves us alone to fight our own battles as we can."*
Charles Kingsley [18]

## HOW TO BUILD A FRIENDSHIP

Here are a few basic principles to use in forging friendships:

1. Develop an attitude of acceptance. Accept your friends as they are - warts and all. "During the Korean war, the phone rang in a fashionable home on the east coast of the United States. To her astonished delight, the woman who answered found herself speaking to her son. There had been long months of silence during his absence in Korea, and now she was both startled and delighted to hear that he was in San Diego, on his way home.

   "Mom, I just wanted to let you know that I'm bringing a buddy home with me. He got hurt pretty bad, and he has only one eye, one arm and one leg. I'd sure like him to live with us."

   "Sure son," she replied. "He sounds like a brave man. We can find room for him for a while."

   "Mom, you don't understand. I want him to come and live with us."

   "Well, O.K." she relented. "We could try it for six months or so."

   "No Mum. I want him to stay always. He needs us. He's only got one arm, one leg and one eye. He's really in bad shape."

   His mother lost patience. "Son, you're being pretty unrealistic about this. You're being emotional because you've been in the war. That boy will be a drag on you and a problem for all of us. Be reasonable."

   Suddenly the phone clicked dead. The next day the parents received from the Navy a telegram that crushed them. The night before, their son had leaped to his death from the twelfth floor of a San Diego hotel. A week later they received the body and looked down with unspeakable sorrow on the corpse of their one-eyed, one-armed, one-legged son." [19]

Conditional acceptance destroys people. Remember God accepts us unconditionally, warts and all.

2. Develop mutual attraction. There are certain people that you will feel you click with.

3. Develop commitment. It seems to me that women in our society, are more skilled at forming deep relationships than men are. However, many men need the security and support that comes from a solid friendship. If you want a deep and lasting friendship, show commitment.

4. Develop genuine openness. I know there will be a risk but the rewards are great. When we open our lives to someone else, we are giving ourselves away and that is costly. But how much more costly is it not to give? Throw away the masks.

Lawrence Peters has noted that you can always tell a real friend by the fact that when you've made a fool of yourself, he doesn't feel you've done a permanent job!

5. Develop appreciation and enjoyment. Delight in the success of your friends. "Friendship doubles our joy and divides our grief." [Anonymous]

## HOW NOT TO CHOOSE A FRIEND

There is a danger that we will open our lives to the wrong kind of people. It simply is not true that we need all the friends we can get.

1. Learn to stand alone. Those who are best equipped for friendship are those most prepared to stand alone. This person is committed to standing firm on his or her convictions, whatever the cost in terms of popularity or social acceptance.

2. Learn to say NO. People are not morally neutral. They either influence our lives for good or bad.

3. Learn who to stay away from:-

a. The Gossip. Avoid the gossip. If they are not loyal to others, they will not be loyal to you.
b. The Quick-Tempered. Proverbs 22:24-25 says, "Do not associate with a man given to anger, or go with a hot-tempered man, lest you learn his way, and find a name for yourself."
c. The Disloyal. Loyalty is one of the greatest virtues in a friendship. Give it and expect it.

*"A friend is one who walks in when others walk out."*
[Walter Winchell]

d. The Discontented. Watch the whiner, the complainer, those who constantly maintain a bad attitude to authority or circumstances.
e. The Self-Indulgent. Keep away from selfish people who are wrapped up in themselves, their wants and wishes.
f. The Immoral. With friends like this, you are on the road to disaster. If they want you to read that dirty book, see the dirty film or listen to the dirty language, you cannot help being affected for the worst.

## THE OTHER SIDE

The choice is yours.

I had the privilege of attending the National Prayer Breakfast in Washington DC. While I was there, I drove past the famous

Watergate buildings and my mind went back to those tragic days during the Nixon administration. He lost the Presidency because he listened to the advice and counsel of untrustworthy men.

The old saying is so very true, "You go like the company you keep". So be sure and choose good friends. They could well make or break you.

A true friend can be one of the most precious things in the world. As a leader, it is so important that you develop a good network of friends.

Yes, it is true, when we lose a friend we die a little.

Henry Penn, former president of the Society of American Florists, tells what he calls one of the most memorable incidents of his life as a florist. One day two boys and a girl about ten years of age made a visit to his store. They wore ragged clothes, but had clean faces and hands. The boys took off their caps when they entered the shop. One of them stepped forward and said solemnly, "We're the committee and we'd like some very nice yellow flowers." Penn showed them some inexpensive spring flowers but the boy said, "I think we'd like something better than that." "Do they have to be yellow?" "Yes sir," was the reply. "Mickey would like it even better if they were yellow because he had a yellow sweater." "Are these for a funeral?" the florist asked quietly. The boy nodded. The girl turned to keep back the tears. "She's his sister," the boy explained. "He was a good kid - a truck - yesterday - he was playing in the street. We saw it happen." Then the other boy added, "Us kids took up a collection. We got eighteen cents."

"Would roses cost an awful lot, Mister? Yellow roses?" Touched by the story of the tragedy and the loyalty and love of these youngsters, Penn replied, "I have some nice yellow roses here that I'm selling for eighteen cents a dozen". "Gee, those would be swell!" exclaimed one of the boys. "Mickey would like those," the other confirmed. "I'll make up a nice spray," promised the sympathetic florist, "with ferns and a ribbon". "Where shall I send them?" "Would it be all right, Mister, if we took 'em now?" asked one of the boys. "We'd kinda like to take 'em over and give 'em to Mickey ourselves. He'd like it better that way." Penn accepted the eighteen cents. The "committee" carrying the kind of flowers "Mickey would like" walked out of the shop. Said Penn, "I felt uplifted for days. Unbeknown to them, I had a part in their tribute to their friend." [20]

In everyone's life, there are basically three levels of relationships: acquaintance, casual, and intimate.

As a leader, develop close friends.

Never underestimate the power of influence. The influence of those around us is so powerful, so subtle, so gradual that often we do not even realize how it can affect us. You cannot afford the luxury of negative associates.

With all your desire for achievement and success, do not forget your friends. John Landy would have to be one of Australia's all time best athletes. Here is the way Gordon Moyes describes his incredible race at the Melbourne 1956 Olympic Games.

"I was present at what I believe will go down in history as the greatest event in Australian athletic history.

It was in 1956, the time of the Melbourne Olympic Games. We saw many fine things at those games. I remember, for example, Vladimir Kutz and his marvellous runs in the five and ten thousand metres, and the great marathon. But it was another race that year which went far beyond anything that happened in the Olympic Games.

Back in 1956 there were only a few athletes around the world who had broken the impenetrable barrier of the four minute mile. In Australia we had the fastest mile runner in the world. No one else could compare with John Landy, who was not only our national champion but was running at that time as world champion.

He was, at this stage, preparing for the race that everyone in athletic circles knew would be the race described as the "race of the century" at the forthcoming Olympic Games. Some of the best runners in the world had come to Australia to tackle Landy. It was the Australian National Athletic Championships held in Melbourne on the new Olympic Park track in January 1956. In the mile race also was the Australian junior mile champion, an eighteen year old, a very fit and fine runner by the name of Ron Clarke.

As the day of the National Championships dawned, everybody was on edge. Landy had been down to 3 minutes 56.6 seconds and we were looking forward to seeing him breaking the four minute mile in this great race. Here were the best mile runners in the world gathered together. The gun went off and they ran the first lap in fifty-nine seconds. Immediately there was a sense of tremendous excitement among the 22,000 spectators: they were under a minute for the first quarter; if only they could maintain two fast middle quarters then the record would tumble. They were past the half-mile in a fast 2 minute 2 seconds. Ron Clarke moved to the front and increased the pace.

John Landy moved up into place behind Ron Clarke. We knew now that the record bid was really on. Everybody at that stage, with half a mile to go, started to chant, "Landy, Landy, Landy!" Around they went and as they moved into the first bend on the third lap an athlete, Alec Henderson, making a fast move, clipped Ron Clarke's heel and Clarke fell over. Landy leapt over the sprawling Clarke. What happened then amazed us. Landy stopped, ran back and picked him up. He said he was sorry. The rest of the runners kept going.

It was his chance for a world record. But Landy picked Clarke up, brushed his knees and looked at the athletes already sixty yards in front; then they both set off after the rest.

I have never heard such a roar from a crowd as I did at that moment. Round the rest of the track, narrowing up, passing first one then another, pegging them back as they moved into the last bend, Landy moved to the front and the crowd was ecstatic. He won! He won in four minutes four seconds. But I tell you, if he had won in three minutes fifty seconds there would not have been a louder cheer than the one that went up that day.

We had witnessed something remarkable. A man at the time of his own opportunity for world fame and recognition gave away his chance in order to pick up another athlete. There was never a more gentlemanly athlete than the one we used to refer to as "Gentleman John". He was the most humble and kindly man I knew: a self-effacing, brilliant man." [21]

The deepest emotional scars develop in the lives of those who feel lonely and rejected. This seems to be a day of superficial friendships. As social beings we all crave acceptance and need the encouragement of friends. We need to constantly strengthen existing friendships and to reach out to others who need caring relationships.

Sundar Singh was a famous Indian preacher who each year journeyed into Tibet. One year, he and two friends were travelling through the high mountains and were caught out in a severe snow storm. After trudging several miles one of his friends dropped exhausted in the snow. The other friend said to Sundar, "We must leave him otherwise we all will perish. I'm going on."

Sundar looked with compassion at his friend lying in the snow then stooped down, picked up the man and threw him over his shoulder and staggered on. Soon after he came across the lifeless form of the other man. He had failed to make it. But Sundar Singh made it through to safety because, as he carried the other man, so the two exchanged body heat, preserving them both.

In his book "Quality Friendship" Gary Inrig writes:
Out of the furnaces of war come many true stories of sacrificial friendship. One such story tells of two friends in World War I, who were inseparable. They had enlisted together, trained together, were shipped overseas together, and fought side-by-side in the trenches. During an attack, one of the men was critically wounded in a field filled with barbed wire obstacles, and he was unable to crawl back to his foxhole. The entire area was under a withering enemy crossfire, and it was suicidal to try to reach him. Yet his friend decided to try. Before he could get out of his own trench, his sergeant yanked him back inside and ordered him not to go. "It's too late. You can't do him any good, and you'll only get yourself killed."

A few minutes later, the officer turned his back, and instantly the man was gone after his friend. A few minutes later he staggered back, mortally wounded, with his friend, now dead, in his arms. The sergeant was both angry and deeply moved. "What a waste," he blurted out. "He's dead and you're dying. It just wasn't worth it."

With almost his last breath, the dying man replied, "Oh, yes it was Sarge. When I got to him the only thing he said was, 'I knew you'd come, Jim!'"

One of the marks of a true friend is that he is there when there is every reason for him not to be, when to be there is sacrificially costly. As Proverbs 17:17 puts it, "A friend loves at all times, and a brother is born for adversity."
[22]

## THE TIME TO MAKE FRIENDS IS BEFORE
## YOU NEED THEM.

Develop a close circle of trusted friends, all sharing a common vision, build into their lives, and grow old together.

8. THE
LEADER
EXERCISES
TACT AND
DIPLOMACY

Don't lead your
team with a
whip, give
them a dream
and help them
reach it.

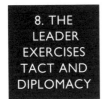

**8. THE LEADER EXERCISES TACT AND DIPLOMACY**

Leadership not only involves knowing where you are going but also how to effectively work with people.

In working together with people, the leader needs warmth, enthusiasm and sensitivity.

## HOW TO EARN THE LOYALTY OF YOUR TEAM

The loyalty of your team is priceless. It cannot be bought or secured by favours. It is not won overnight. It is not everlasting. Loyalty is only given by your team as they think their leader is worthy of it.

Effective leaders make their team feel good about themselves and their work.

Here are some ways to gain and hold the loyalty of people:

1. Help people be successful in THEIR jobs. Give and do everything you possibly can in helping your team to achieve their goals.

a. Provide training. Most work is badly done because of poor or inadequate training. Encourage extra courses and study. Send them to that seminar. Provide teaching tapes and videos. Focus on "continuous improvement" rather than "static perfection".
b. Get extra help when needed. Insufficient help will hinder performance.
c. Provide the best equipment you possibly can. This will ensure that they do their work more effectively.
d. Look for ways to help them yourself. The personal touch, even though at times may be inconvenient, will prove you care for them personally.
e. Provide the best possible working environment. Environment determines attitude, and attitude determines altitude. The better the surroundings, the better they will feel about their work and themselves. It was a wise person who said, "It's not the mountain ahead that bothers the climber, but the grain of sand in the shoe."

f. Resolve minor complaints or concerns before they become major ones. As a leader you must look after the needs of your team.

*"What we have done for ourselves alone dies with us. What we have done for others and the world remains and is immortal."*
Albert Pine

2. Learn to confide in people you can trust. An individual feels important and special when information is shared.

3. Recognize and show appreciation for all the team. It is not just the high achievers but the consistent plodders that need encouragement. Be proud of the accomplishments of your team. Always give them credit for their successes. Meet with them personally or contact them by phone. Encourage them to share their heart. People thrive on the appreciation you show them - the smiles, the thanks, and the gestures of kindness. Be on the lookout for those things that are done well. Praise and recognition are powerful motivators.

4. Keep your word. Don't break a promise. Soon you will lose the loyalty of everyone.

5. Be patient. Do not give up on a person until ample opportunity has been given for improvement. Try to always give them the benefit of the doubt.

6. Reward performance. Unselfishly given well-deserved credit to your people is one of the finest things you can do for them. It not only makes them feel good but stimulates them to try even harder. Write letters to those who deserve credit, they in turn will show these to their friends and family.

Knowing your team is so important. The praise and reward must be carefully chosen to suit each individual. What motivates one person may not motivate another. The rewards may include promotion, trips, salary increase, the knowledge of job security, plaques or gifts. Use your wisdom and imagination to make life a little more exciting for others.

The best way to gain and hold the loyalty of your team is to show personal interest in them and care for them, by your words and actions, in everything you do. Be sincere in doing everything in your power to help them succeed as a team and as an individual.

## LEADERS STUDY AND KNOW PEOPLE

The study of people and their various temperaments is fascinating. Just as snowflakes have different designs so have people been given distinguishing qualities of uniqueness.

Temperament provides men and women with both strengths and weaknesses. Although we like to think only of our strengths, everyone has weaknesses.

Dr. Tim LaHaye and Florence Littauer have produced several very good books that will help you as a leader to better understand how people think and function.

Basically, they are saying that everyone is a curious mixture of weaknesses and strengths. The reason is that everyone has inherited a distinct temperament - predominantly sanguine, choleric, melancholy, or phlegmatic, with a combination of traits from two or more groups.

| EXTROVERT | |
|---|---|
| **SANGUINE** POPULAR FUN WAY | **CHOLERIC** POWERFUL MY WAY |
| **PHLEGMATIC** PEACEFUL EASY WAY | **MELANCHOLY** PERFECT RIGHT WAY |
| INTROVERT | |

Let's look at these temperaments in a little more detail:

## 1. THE SANGUINE

This person is often the warm, popular "fun way" type. He is the buoyant, lively temperament. Feelings predominate to form his decisions rather than reflective thoughts.

| Sanguine Strengths | Sanguine Weaknesses |
|---|---|
| Talkative | Weak-willed |
| Outgoing | Unstable |
| Enthusiastic | Undisciplined |
| Warm | Egocentric |
| Personable | Loud |
| Friendly | Exaggerates |
| Compassionate | Fearful |
| Carefree | Restless |
| | Undependable |

These people are usually actors, salespeople, speakers.

## 2. THE CHOLERIC

These people are the hot, quick, active, practical, and strong-willed temperament. Often self-sufficient, and very independent. They tend to be decisive and opinionated, finding it easy to make decisions for themselves and for other people. To them, "life is activity". They are often domineering and bossy. They can use people.

| Choleric Strengths | Choleric Weaknesses |
|---|---|
| Strong-willed | Angry |
| Determined | Cruel |
| Independent | Sarcastic |
| Optimistic | Domineering |
| Practical | Inconsiderate |
| Productive | Proud |
| Decisive | Self-sufficient |
| Leader | Unemotional |
| Confident | Crafty |

These type of people are usually producers, builders, and leaders.

## 3. THE PHLEGMATIC

This person has the calm, cool, slow, easy-going, well-balanced temperament. They rarely get ruffled no matter what the circumstances. They tend to be a spectator in life and try not to get too involved in the activity of others. Generally they will not take leadership on their own but when it is put on them, they prove a capable leader.

| Phlegmatic Strengths | Phlegmatic Weaknesses |
|---|---|
| Calm | |
| Stingy | |
| Easy-going | Fearful |
| Dependable | Indecisive |
| Efficient | Spectator |
| Conservative | Self-protective |
| Practical | Selfish |
| Leader | Unmotivated |
| Diplomat | |
| Humourous | |

These people are usually diplomats, accountants, teachers, and technicians.

## 4. THE MELANCHOLY

This type of person is usually a perfectionist. They are analytical, self-sacrificing, and gifted with a very sensitive emotional nature. Although they don't make friends easily, they prove to be very faithful as a friend. They can often experience a variety of moods because their feelings predominate.

| Melancholy Strengths | Melancholy Weaknesses |
| --- | --- |
| Gifted | Self-centred |
| Analytical | Moody |
| Sensitive | Negative |
| Perfectionist | Theoretical |
| Aesthetic | Impractical |
| Idealistic | Unsociable |
| Loyal | Critical |
| Self-sacrificing | Revengeful |
| | Rigid [23] |

The Melancholies are usually artists, musicians, inventors, philosophers and professors.

Although the theory of these four temperaments are not perfect, and no concept of man is, it does, however, help the average person to examine themselves and those they associate with.

Wise leaders concentrate on their strengths and overcome their weaknesses. As a leader, you should help your team to develop their strengths and overcome their weaknesses as well. The knowledge of these temperaments is just a tool to help you deal with, and appreciate people more. But, like any tool, it can be misused. We must continue to see people as people and not go around analysing everyone we meet, putting them into our own pigeonholes.

## THE LEADER IS AN ENCOURAGER

The most important responsibility of a leader is to develop your team. Your success as a leader is dependent on how well your team performs.

Everyone has an invisible sign hanging from their neck that reads, "Make me feel important!" Never forget this message when working with people.

## A SUCCESSFUL TEAM BEATS WITH ONE HEART.

If you don't teach people how to fish, they will certainly learn on their own how to steal your fish.

*"There is no exercise better for the heart than reaching down and lifting people up."*
John A Holmes

Any organization that is not growing and developing is stagnating. As growth occurs, mistakes will be made. It is at this point that the leaders prove themselves by their reactions. Accept honest mistakes as the price for innovation. The attitude must be - what can we learn? Mistakes can become stepping stones to success. If your team is not making a mistake or two it's a sure sign they are playing it too safe.

As a leader you must create the kind of climate in your organization where personal growth is expected, recognized and rewarded. Encourage your team to explore new options instead of settling for the obvious.

One cause of depression in people is the hunger for appreciation and encouragement. I remember reading one of Chuck Swindoll's newsletters where he told of the geese that fly in V-formation, honking as they make their way to a warmer climate, covering thousands of miles before they reach their destination. He noted these observations:

1. Those in front rotate their leadership. When one goose gets tired, it changes place with the one in the wing on the V-formation and another flies point.

2. By flying as they do the members of the flock create an upward air current for one another. Each flap of the wings literally creates an uplift for the bird immediatly following. One author

states that by flying in a V-formation the whole flock gets 71 percent greater flying range than if each goose flew on its own.

3. When one goose gets sick or wounded two fall out of formation with it and follow it down to help and protect it. They stay with the struggler until its able to fly again.

4. The geese in the rear of the formation are the ones who do the honking. I suppose its their way of announcing that they're following and all is well. For sure repeated honks encourage those in front to stay with it." [24]

Leaders today need to continue their honks of encouragement. Catch your people doing something right and let them know about it. Seek them out when they are down and build them up again.

Mary Kay Ash, founder and president of Mary Kay Cosmetics would say, "Forget their mistakes and zero in on one small thing they do right. Praise them and they'll do more things right and discover talents and abilities they never realised they had."

*"There is no more noble occupation in the world than to assist another human being - to help someone succeed."*
{Alan Loy McGinnis, Bringing Out The Best In People]

*"A good boss is one who makes people think they have more ability than they have so they consistently do better work than they thought they could".* [Charles E Wilson, former CEO of General Motors]

At one time, Andrew Carnegie was the wealthiest man in America. He came to America from his native Scotland when he was a small boy, did a variety of odd jobs and eventually ended up as the largest steel manufacturer in the United States. At one time he had forty-three millionaires working for him. In those days, a millionaire was a rare person; conservatively speaking a million dollars in his day would be equivalent to at least twenty million dollars today.

A reporter asked Carnegie how he had hired forty-three millionaires. Carnegie responded that those men had not been millionaires when they started working for him, but had become millionaires as a result.

The reporter's next question was, "How did you develop these men to become so valuable to you that you have paid them this much money?" Carnegie replied that "Men are developed the same way gold is mined. When gold is mined, several tons of dirt must be moved to get an ounce of gold; but one doesn't go into the mine looking for dirt - one goes in looking for the gold."

*And remember, "It takes two wings for a bird to fly".*
Jessie Jackson

So, as a leader, build a powerful team.

Innovation creates opportunity, quality creates demand, but it takes team work to make it happen.

Don't lead your team with a whip, give them a dream and help them reach it.

**9. THE LEADER DEVELOPS EXECUTIVE ABILITY**

—

To build a
better
dream, you
must build a
better you.

**9. THE LEADER DEVELOPS EXECUTIVE ABILITY**

To build a better dream, you must build a better you.

Successful leaders recognise that developing leadership skills is a lifetime pursuit. In their study of ninety top leaders in all fields, Bennis and Nanus found, "It is the capacity to develop and improve their skills that distinguishes leaders from their followers". The researchers also came to the conclusion that "leaders are perpetual learners".

The people who succeed are those who have the self-discipline to develop themselves. Successful leaders never plateau or become static. Effective leaders are not satisfied with themselves. They have the courage to discover their shortocmings.

Leaders learn to be leaders. The development of leadership skills is a never-ending process. A leader never "arrives".

*"Unless you try to do something beyond what you already have mastered, you will never grow."*
Ronald Osborn

Those who will not take the time and the trouble to keep up-to-date in our competitive society will be left behind. The extent of knowledge is doubling every two years. Soon it will be even faster. If you do not think about the future and prepare for it you may not have one.

What you are becoming is far more important than what you get. What you become directly influences what you get. You must work harder on yourself than you do on your job. Income rarely exceeds personal development. Your life will change only when you change.

Each leader develops his/her own individual "style". As you develop as a leader it is so important that you keep in mind your vision, your goals and dreams. There is something magnetic about people who know where they are going in life. Good feelings and positive energy radiate from such people.

Here are some suggestions for self-development:

1. Study the techniques of successful leaders. Carefully observe how they articulate a vision of the future and how they inspire others to achieve it. Adopt the successful approaches that you feel comfortable with.

*"Cultivate in yourself the qualities you admire most in others."*
Arnold Glason

2. Live in balance. We live in a crazy, rat-race world. It is so important for a leader to keep a balance in their life. Everything you do affects the other areas of your life. It's like a coin. You can spend it anyway you want but you can only spend it once.

Here are seven basic areas of life that you need to keep in balance. They are like the spokes of a wheel. Make one longer or shorter and the whole wheel is out of balance.

* Family and marriage
* Financial
* Personal growth
* Physical
* Professional
* Social
* Spiritual

You may need to spend some quiet, quality time going over these areas. What have you been neglecting or what have you been spending too much time, energy or money on? You may have to seek out some good trusted friends to help restore your sense of balance.

3. Maintain confidence. All leaders, at some time in their lives, doubt themselves and their ability. If you haven't, get ready, at some time it will come. Many in executive or leadership positions question their own competence at some time. Your vision starts to get a little hazy and out of focus.

Self-development is so important because it helps you to maintain your self-confidence. When you stagnate, you tend to lose confidence.

Identify your greatest strength and maximize it.

Reflect on your past success for future victory. David did this before he fought the giant Goliath. He remembered how he defeated the bear and the lion. God encouraged the Israelites to remember how He opened the Red Sea to give them confidence to take possession of the Promised Land.

Seek out some trusted friends for support, encouragement and advice.

Watch out for self-centredness. Remember, true leadership is serving others. So many depend on the attention or the recognition or the affirmation of the crowd. Without it they become anxious. Focus on the needs of others.

Get back to the focus of your vision. Read it over and over again. Focus on what you truly want to do and be in the future.

### THE CONFIDENT PERSON INSPIRES LEADERSHIP.

4. Leaders develop creativity. Need is the mother of creativity. There is very little that can stand against the pressure of sustained thought. You must constantly ask the question, "How can I or we do it better?"

You are far more creative than you think you are.

THE 10 LAWS OF LEADERSHIP

*"I have no special gift - I am only passionately curious"*
Albert Einstein

Force yourself to have think-tank sessions to stimulate your creative abilities.

5. Leaders keep renewing their self-motivation. Motivation is the key to successful living. Leaders motivate themselves to take positive, goal-orientated action.

How do you attain and maintain success?

First you need the WISDOM to know what to do.
Second, the KNOWLEDGE of how to do it.
and Third, the SELF-MOTIVATION to do it.

There are two parts to motivating yourself.
a. Mental: you conceive in your mind where you want to go.
b. Physical: you take action to get there.

### SELF-MOTIVATION - THOUGHT AND ACTION - IS THE KEY TO SUCCESS.

As you observe a leader you will notice that as soon as they achieve a goal they will set newer and higher goals. There will be disappointments and failures but they learn how to overcome them and go on to further success.

The fires of motivation are fed by the fuel of dreams. If you feel like you are slowing down, or have lost touch, get back to your dreams, your goals, and your vision. Go over them again and get them clearly set in your mind. Don't get sidetracked, snowed-under, or fatigued. Try to clearly assess what is causing the problem and rectify it immediately. Find a person that you are accountable to for help if necessary. The key is to get back to your original dream, your vision.

6. Leaders control stress. The pressures on twentieth century man are incredible. Meeting deadlines, phone calls, traffic lights, and high prices are just a few of the things that cause pressure. The spin-offs are overwhelming - depression, stress, loss of happiness, worry, care and anxiety. The leader feels them all.

A certain amount of stress is important for life to have meaning. Stress is necessary for us to have happy, productive lives. Without some stress, we become easily bored and lack direction. This is often the problem of the newly retired executive. The key is to function with a level of stress that is life enhancing - not life threatening.

It is not the single stressful event that harms people, but the long term stress built up at an increasingly higher, uninterrupted level.

According to the American Medical Association,"80% of our diseases are either caused or aggravated by stress." [Bottom Line-Personal, April 30, 1984] These diseases range from minor ailments (eg., aches and pains) to life-threatening diseases (eg., strokes, heart attacks, ulcers and cancer). Stress can even weaken one's immune system.

Here are some practical principles to help you cope with stress:

a. Go back to basics.
    Stop and answer some blunt questions:
    * Are you getting enough sleep?
    * Is your diet adequate and balanced?
    * Are you taking time to relax?
    * Are you neglecting your family?
    * Are you keeping in contact with close friends?
    * Are you simply trying to do too much?

Very often most problems can be solved with us having just a few early nights! Take time to clearly analyse the physical and social areas of your life.

b. Confide in a trusted friend. Leaders need friends. We must find a trusted confidant who will be honest with us. ("Faithful are the wounds of a friend"). We need someone who will listen, advise, pray and help us to see life objectively again, life in it's true perspective. We need friends to preserve our integrity and often our sanity!

c. Take off the mask. We need to make a clear decision to stop pretending to be what we are not. It takes a great deal of effort to maintain an image. Start being yourself and the stress level will start to fall.

Be yourself - but be your "best self".

d. Learn to laugh. A good sense of humour is one of the most priceless gifts in the world. If you have not got a good sense of humour, you may be in for real trouble.

Try not to take yourself so seriously. Don't be so intense about everything.

Laughter is a marvellous answer to stress and pressure. It may be time to let your hair down - if you have enough!

So often we think God is a kill-joy boss who begrudges every moment not at work.

It might be good to sit down with your kids and read some of their comics with them.

There is an old Greek motto that says:
You will break the bow if you keep it always bent.

So why don't you -

* Go out and have a good fun time and don't you dare feel guilty about it afterwards.

* Block out some leisure time in your diary to ensure you'll take some days off for refreshment and relaxation.

When fun fades, laughter leaves. We are left uptight with the making of a coronary. Don't lose your humour - keep laughing.

e. Determine what really is vital and important. We must try to determine the root cause of our stress, tensions and pressure. We need to identify where we are vulnerable. Much of our pressure can be avoided.

Maybe we need to change our priorities:
* Could someone else do what causes our pressure?
* Could better planning help?
* What committees should we give up?
* What clubs do we really have to belong to?
* What meetings should we stop attending?

What are our real priorities? The crazy rat race we live today can crowd out what is really important. If we are not ruthless with ourselves and take the time (and it will take time) to determine what is vital, then the pressure and stress will continue to mount up. If things have reached such a pitch for you, then take time right now to sort things out.

### WORK SMARTER - NOT HARDER.

Stop trying to cover all the bases and sell popcorn in the stands at the same time!

f. If you need it - get help. Medical help may be needed. You may feel this is an admission of failure but it is nothing of the kind. The mind is a very delicate and complex thing. Today it seems so acceptable to visit a doctor with a broken arm but not a broken heart.

g. Maintain good health habits. To be really effective as a leader you must keep yourself in good shape. So many good leaders suffer with their health because they fail to discipline themselves. Take a trip to any shopping mall and observe the physical condition of the people who parade by. Here are a few areas the leader needs to constantly work on:

* Exercise. Jogging, swimming, aerobic walking and gym work all help to keep you in shape.

Remember that when you exercise it is important to:-

1. Warm up prior to strenuous exercise. There are a number of stretching exercises needed. Read a good book on the subject.

2. Start slowly and work up. The first few weeks of exercise need to be gradually introduced. It may be advisable to visit your doctor for advice first.

3. After exercising, take a few minutes to cool down. This step is so often forgotten because of our hectic pace. Go through your stretching exercises again.

* Keep your weight down.
* Minimize the amount of fat consumed in your diet.
* Don't use too much salt.
* Get regular sleep.
* Keep the caffeine intake down.

A flood of evidence have been produced to show these habits are detrimental to good health. But make sure that you keep everything in balance. Enjoy life, moderation is the key.

* Nutrition and diet. Your body is in a constant state of change and needs good nourishment. Get some good advice on nutrition. Watch the overuse of sugar. Leaders, because they use

up energy, need a well balanced vitamin intake. Experimer get some good advice as to what is best for you.

* Invest in a regular medical checkup.

* Ensure recreation time is not overlooked. All work and no play does make Johnny a dull boy. You need to be re-created constantly. Annual holidays and mini-holidays are essential to keep you on an even keel. A walk in the park at lunchtime, doing something crazy and unexpected will add zest and vigour to your life. Have you ever heard anyone on their death bed say: "I wish I'd spent more time at the office"?

* Think on good things. Deliberately put out of your mind the unpleasant and ugly experiences of life and force yourself to think about pleasant, uplifting thoughts, the beauty around you, the good, the right, the beautiful.

Your executive ability occurs only when you have a pool of energy to draw from. Therefore, your success will depend on your health, your fitness, your mental well-being, and the amount of rest you get.

*"A man too busy to take care of his health is like a mechanic too busy to take care of his tools."*
Spanish Proverb

7. The leader learns how to communicate effectively. No one can be a successful leader who does not endeavour to communicate effectively. The ability to communicate is a must for good leadership. It is not always easy, but you must be persistent. Effort and persistence will pay. Good communicators often become great leaders. Work at good thoughtful communication. It's true, a boss says, "Get going!" A leader says, "Let's go!"

How to communicate effectively:

1. Get to the point quickly and directly. Don't beat around the bush. Plan ahead what you wish to say and keep it simple.
2. Check your attitude. Be pleasant with people.
3. Treat people with respect. Don't be rude.
4. Criticism will get you nowhere. People will only resist your leading.
5. Don't take people for granted. Treat each person as special.
6. Listen. Use not only your ears but your eyes as well. It's often not so much what we say but how we say it.
7. Ask questions. This ensures that the message is received correctly.
8. Improve your speech. Listen to a tape of you speaking. You may have to dust off an old English language book, or study someone with a pleasant voice. If you are really serious you may even get some lessons like Eliza Dolittle in "My Fair Lady"! People may discount your ability to lead if your diction is poor.

*"There is a relationship - an almost uncanny relationship - which exists between a man's income, and his ability, and his language. Words are tools, and the more tools we have, the more jobs we can handle."*
Earl Nightingale

Make communication an ongoing study, your life-long passion and disipline. Through effective communication, you will out-achieve others who may be more intelligent or have more personality, but who have not developed their communication abilities.

## THE LEADER MUST BE A GOOD COMMUNICATOR.

8. Make your appearance an asset. To act right you have to look right and feel right.

Be well groomed. Make your appearance an asset - not a liability. Do you buy the torn top newspaper on the pile or the one further down? Do you select a nice apple in the shop or a pitted one?

People are looking for the best. Your appearance communicates volumes to people.

You have only one chance at a good first impression.

It is to your advantage to make a good first impression. If you are well dressed, it adds to your self confidence. How do you know what to wear? The key is appropriateness. You wouldn't wear what you wear to the beach to a business meeting. Read up on dress in a good book. [John T. Molloy's, "New Dress For Success", Warner Books, is excellent]. Knowing what suits you best, your best colours etc., will save you a lot of time and money. Shop around. They needn't cost the earth but make sure your clothes are clean and pressed. Keep your shoes clean, polished and in good repair. Good grooming starts from the shoes up. Keep your nails clean and trimmed. If you wear them, keep your glasses clean.

I know it is a free world and you can wear and look how you like but, like it or not, man looks on the outward appearance. So make your appearance work for you. Hair, regardless of style, should be clean and washed. When you look good, you feel good and you act good. Study someone that has good dress sense. Perhaps they can help you with some good advice. Remember that even Jesus looked smart in His dress. When He came to the cross the soldiers divided His clothes and rather than cut up His cloak, they cast lots for it. It must have been valuable and He must have looked good in His dress presentation.

9. The leader's deportment. How you carry yourself is so important. It conveys to people whether or not you are in charge of the situation, that you know where you are going or just your whole attitude to life. Body language is developing into a real science today. Body language is the art of seeing what others are thinking. Manage your own body movements in order to maximize your leadership skills.

10. Think success. Learn to think big. Petty minded people never really succeed in life. The mind is the most delicate, the most sensitive instrument in all creation. Just as the body is what the body is fed, in the same way the mind is what the mind is fed.

Where your thoughts are is the direction you are going in life, up or down.

11. Leaders never stop learning. There is a story of a woman who had been a school teacher for 25 years. When she heard about a job that would mean a promotion she applied for the position. However, someone who had been teaching for only one year was hired instead. She went to the Principal and asked why. The Principal responded, "I'm sorry, but you haven't had 25 years of experience as you claim; you've had only one year's experience 25 times." During that whole time the teacher had not improved.

Howard Hendricks shares this insight about the value of learning: When I was a college student - I worked in the college dining hall and on my way to work at 5.30 every morning I walked past the home of one of my professors. Through a window I could see the light on at his desk, morning after morning.

At night I stayed late at the library to take advantage of evening study hours, and returning home at 10.30 or 11 o'clock I would again see his desk light on. He was always pouring over his books.

One day he invited me home for lunch, and after the meal I said to him, "Would you mind if I asked you a question?"

"Of course not."

"What keeps you studying? You never seem to stop."

His answer, "Son, I would rather have my students drink from a running stream than a stagnant pool."

12. Maintain your standards. Always remember - your greatest asset as you develop your executive ability is your character quality. This is what will shine through above all else. True character is what a person is like when they are alone. You must learn to live by the highest standards of honesty and integrity. Every time people engage in dishonest or immoral acts, the results come back to haunt them. Always ask yourself, "Is this the right thing to do?" The development of highly-principled leaders is vitally important to the future of any organisation. It is imperative for the future of any country. The greatest example you can leave your followers as a leader is your standard of honesty and integrity. With integrity, some day you will be able to look back on your accomplishments with pride and satisfaction.

The most important quality to your success as a leader is INTEGRITY.

*"In reading the lives of great men, I found that the first victory they won was over themselves."*
Harry S. Truman

**10. THE
LEADER EXUDES
INSPIRATIONAL
POWER**

Leaders
have a sense
of purpose,
and destiny.

10. THE LEADER EXUDES INSPIRATIONAL POWER

Most leaders don't just enter a room, they seem to invade a room!

What is it that seems to set leaders apart? What certain qualities do they possess that makes them different? What is it that people admire in them that causes them to want to follow their leadership?

What leadership qualities did Napoleon have? When he was retreating from Moscow, his army of 600,000 were either killed, captured, deserted or died of illness leaving only 100,000 remaining. Still his men showed such loyalty for the Emperor that, even while he slept, they threw their own coats over him to keep him warm while they endured the sub-zero temperatures.

Leaders inspire, create commitment, act as role models and evoke the highest level of commitment and competence possible from their team.

Many leaders make the mistake of causing people to feel reverence for their leader. Exceptional leaders induce their team to feel reverence for themselves.

What are some of the qualities in a leader that create inspiration in others and causes them to work together, as a team, under the leader's direction, in order to attain a common objective? Just what is it that makes people want to follow the leader's lead?

1. Leaders have a sense of purpose. Leaders know where they are going.

*"Men fail through lack of purpose rather than through lack of talent."*
Billy Sunday

The world steps aside for the person who knows where they are going. It was Charles Kingsley who said, "I go at what I have to do as if there was nothing else in the world for me to do." Again it was Benjamin Disraeli who stated, "The secret of success is constancy to purpose."

This sense of purpose, of direction, is clearly evident in real leaders; and because of this there is a sense of urgency in what they do. They want to do something and they want to do it NOW. People who keep hustling are in great demand in organizations. If there is one thing a leader should fear it is complacency.

*"Even though you're on the right track - you'll get run over if you just sit there!"*
Will Rogers

2. Leaders are enthusiastic. This energy of enthusiasm attracts attention. Enthusiasm attracts followers. Enthusiasm will gain the acceptance and confidence of others. Enthusiasm creates excitement.

Leaders exude this energy of enthusiasm. You can sense it in them. It demonstrates itself in vitality. It creates mental alertness, hard work and persistence.

## ENTHUSIASM IS LIKE THE FIZZ IN THE LEMONADE.

The power of enthusiasm is fantastic. It's like grease on the axle of a wheel, it smoothes your journey to your goals. People will respond to your excitement.

Enthusiasm requires daring. The world belongs to the person who is enthusiastic about life.

"Enthusiasm changes problems to challenges.
Enthusiasm creates enthusiasm in others.

Enthusiasm rids the mind of worry and tension.
Enthusiasm improves your outlook on life.
Enthusiasm forgets yesterday and attacks today.
So - think enthusiastically." [24]

3. Leaders demonstrate determination. High-performing leaders exhibit exceptional determination in pursuing their objectives, they never let up until they succeed. As you make a study of great leaders you will notice their remarkable determination. Often against all odds they will persist until they reach their goals.

*"Nothing in the world can take the place of persistence. Talent will not - nothing is more common than unsuccessful men with talent. Genius will not - rewarded genius is a proverb. Education will not - the world is full of educated derelicts. Persistence and determination alone are omnipotent."*
Calvin Coolidge

Determination is like a postage stamp; its usefulness consists in the ability to stick to one thing until it gets there!

An executive at one time was taken down a peg. "You may well feel proud of yourself young man," he said to the life insurance agent. "I've refused to see seven insurance men today". "I know", said the agent, "I'm them!"

The Five "D's" to Success are:

   * DESIRE
   * DETERMINATION
   * DEDICATION
   * DISCIPLINE
   * DRIVE
The Sixth "D" - DISTRACTION - is to be avoided at all costs.

When you think you are at the end of your rope, tie a knot in it and hang on! The person who gets ahead, is the one who does more than is necessary - and keeps on doing it.

"Teddy Roosevelt had one trait that overshadowed everything else: determination. As a child he was small, had poor eyesight and suffered from severe asthma. In his autobiography Roosevelt noted that he often lay in bed struggling to breathe, afraid that he would not awaken in the morning. Weakened by his illness, he had to rely on Elliot, his younger brother, to shield him from the neighbourhood bullies."

"Nevertheless, Teddy willed himself to become strong both mentally and physically. Each day he pushed himself; he spent hours lifting weights and doing chin-ups. Interested in a wide variety of subjects, he read every book he could get his hands on. By the time he enrolled at Harvard, Roosevelt had become a man of extreme energy and enthusiasm. Faculty and students alike described him as being forceful and colourful." [25]

*"The longer I live, the more deeply am I convinced that that which makes the difference between one man and another - between the weak and the powerful, the great and the insignificant, is energy - invisible determination - a purpose once formed, and then death or victory. This quality will do anything that is to be done in the world; and no talents, no circumstances, no opportunities will make one a man without it."*
Buxton

Helen Keller, despite her blindness, graduated from Radcliffe College in 1904; a tough assignment even for a normal person. She finished with excellent reading knowledge of Greek, Latin, German and French - all in braille of course. Some years later Woodrow Wilson asked her why she had chosen Radcliffe when she could have selected an easier college. "Because they didn't want me at Radcliffe," she answered, "and, being stubborn, I chose to override their objection." Helen Keller had determination plus.

Hugh Sidney, writing in "Time" magazine, describes George Washington's role at the Battle of Trenton as follows:

"Three columns were to have crossed the Delaware River; only Washington made it across. The powder of his troops was soaked by freezing rain, so they could not use their arms. They had to defend with bayonets several times during the night, Washington's officers pleaded with him to call off the attack. The story goes that he stood on an old beehive in a muddy New Jersey field and turned aside every petition to retreat. The Battle of Trenton was won by the determination of one man." [26]

Yet all the determination in the world is useless unless your timing is right. You need to know when to put your plan into action or when people are psychologically ready to accept your plans or ideas. The secret is determination with correct timing.

4. Leaders care for their team. A true leader shows genuine love, care and concern for those they lead. You become successful by helping others become successful.

"When you meet a man, you judge him by his clothes.

When you leave a man, you judge him by his heart."
(an old Russian Proverb)

Like it or not, leadership is dealing with people. If you refuse to develop the necessary skills to work with people you will never be a leader. John D. Rockefeller stated, "I will pay more for the ability to deal with people than any other ability under the sun." If you want to lead, you must develop your people skills.

Genuine love for others is a critical component for a leader. If you truly show care, concern and love for others they will easily look past your shortcomings. If they sense that you don't really care for them, then they will be judgemental of everything you do.

A person too busy to take care of his co-workers is like a mechanic too busy to take care of his tools.

*"People want to be appreciated, not impressed. They want to be regarded as human beings, not as sounding boards for other people's egos. They want to be treated as an end in themselves, not as a means towards the gratification of another's vanity."*
Sydney J. Harris

The greatest satisfaction in leadership is that of building people; not in using people to accomplish your goals. To see someone grow and develop as you guide them will be so satisfying as you look back with the perspective of years.

Coming together is a beginning, staying together is progress and working together is success in teamwork.

If you are too busy to help those around you to succeed - you're too busy.

Here are some keys for caring:

1. Give encouragement. Give them hope for the future. "You did a great job." "You're going to make it." Lack of encouragement is the biggest cause of turnover. It is the reason why so many kids leave home, couples divorce, and employees leave organisations. What they are really saying is, "They didn't really encourage me." I'm not talking about hype or false hope but genuine heartfelt encouragement. Help them realise their potential. Give them hope for the future.

2. Show appreciation. Say thank you - often. "I really appreciated the way you helped out." "Thanks for getting that job done so quickly."

Praise loudly, blame softly. Praise in public, discipline in private.

3. Constantly affirm. Encourage personal strengths. "You handled that speech well." "I really appreciate the way you care for people."

4. Remember to recognise. Be aware of your team's accomplishments. "You did a great job on that letter." "You are building a great team."

Your family, friends and team all need your love and encouragement. Few other strengths are as important to the leader as that of building up others.

Every person deserves to, and needs to, know how their leader feels about his or her performance. Build on their strengths. Imagine them in ten or twenty years time. How can you develop their full potential?

### LOVE PEOPLE AND USE THINGS - DON'T LOVE THINGS AND USE PEOPLE.

*"The greatest good you can do for another is not just share your riches, but reveal to him his own."*
Benjamin Disraeli

Always remember - people support what they help create.

*5. Leaders have future focus. Where does your mind mostly dwell - on the past, present or the future?*
The secret of leadership, I believe, is the ability of a leader to continually focus on the future. This is what gives the leader a sense of destiny. They have discovered the purpose for their life and are giving themselves wholly to it.

"There is no sadder sight than a young pessimist."

Mark Twain

A ship in a harbour is safe, but that is not what ships are built for. Leaders are always looking to the future. They accomplish in proportion to what they attempt.

Leaders have two important characteristics:

First - They are going somewhere; and

Second - They are able to persuade other people to go with them.

Those who have a future focus are far more positive and therefore more attractive.

I heard the story recently of a cathedral in England that needed the high ceiling timbers replaced. Where were they to get such timber from? It was a mammoth task. Someone then had the idea of investigating the old church papers and discovered that years ago the then reigning King had ordered that a forest of trees be planted so that there would be timber for replacement in the future. To their amazement the forest was still standing. Upon hearing the story, a leader made the comment, "I wonder if they have planted another forest?" Now there is a leader with future focus.

People will rally to a leader who has future focus because they have a sense of destiny. If you are living in the present you will be constantly critical. If you live in the past, you will tend to be melancholy. If you live with future focus your energy level is higher, your attitude is positive and there will be an attractiveness about you that people will admire and want to follow.

The difference between doing and dabbling is focus.

Expect to win.

## LEADERS OF THE FUTURE

The future has never been filled with greater challenges. To meet these challenges will require that we raise up a new breed of leaders. While principles are timeless, methods need to be under constant review. Here are some of the things that leaders of the future will have to be aware of:

1. Learn to be willing to unlearn. There may be behaviours and techniques that have served you well in the past but may no longer be productive. Leaders of today are entering a future of rapid change and demands.

2. Leaders of the future must be willing to venture into the unknown, for the biggest risk is the unwillingness to take risks. Recognise the danger of safety.

3. Leaders will need to become and remain well informed. They will need to develop the ability to effectively communicate. A major problem that we have now is a breakdown in communications. The most frequent cause of stress in families and organisations is a breakdown in communication between well-intentioned people without the skill to avoid the difficulties.

4. Leaders will need to learn to live in balance. Leaders will need to show the principles of, not just making a living, but making a life.

The future is upon us and it promises to bring drastic, unforseen alterations. Leaders committed to change, learning and excellence can create winners in a climate of change. We do not owe our people a brighter future, but rather we owe our future brighter people.

The Chinese ideogram for crisis contains two characters meaning "danger" and "opportunity". Without good leadership in our world, the future is filled with danger. With good leadership I believe the future will be filled with the greatest opportunities man has ever known.

Together we can change the world.

Are you developing all your potential to be more competent and prepared for the future? The issue is not, can you be an exceptional leader..? The issue is, will you?

Will you?

# FOOTNOTES

[1] K Dyer, *Unity, Leadership, Change & Vision,* (Prospect Heights: K Dyer) (P.63)

[2] *Bible Illustrator,* (Cedar Rapids: Parsons Technology, 1990)

[3] J Haggai, *Lead On,* (Word: Word Books, 1986) (P.27)

[4] *Bible Illustrator* (Cedar Rapids: Parsons Technology, 1990)

[5] *"Success Magazine"* July/August, (New York: Lang Communications, 1989) (P.44)

[6] *Bible Illustrator,* (Cedar Rapids: Parsons Technology, 1990)

[7] *Bible Illustrator*

[8] *Bible Illustrator*

[9] *Bible Illustrator*

[10] *Bible Illustrator*

[11] *Bible Illustrator*

[12] *"World Book Encyclopaedia" Volume 'N',* (Ohio: Field Enterprises, 1976) (P.114)

[13] *"World Book Encyclopaedia" Volume 'N'*

[14] *Bible Illustrator,* (Cedar Rapids; Parsons Technology, 1990)

[15] *Bible Illustrator*

[16] F A Manske, Jr, *Secrets of Effective Leadership,* (Columbia: Leadership Education & Development, Inc. 1987) (P113-130)

[17] *Bible Illustrator,* (Cedar Rapids: Parsons Technology, 1990)

[18] Bill Newman, *The Power of a Successful Life,* (Toowong; BNC Publications, (P.59) 1992)

[19] G Inrig, *Quality Friendships,* (Chicago: Moody Press, 1981) (P.52)

[20] *Bible Illustrator,* (Cedar Rapids: Parsons Technology, 1990)

[21] G Moyes, *Twelve Steps to Serenity,* (Sydney: Hodder & Stoughton, 1985) (P.54)

[22] G Inrig, *Quality Friendships,* (Chicago: Moody Press, 1981) (P.73-74)

[23] T La Haye, *Spirit Controlled Temperament,* (Wheaton, Tyndale, 1966) (P13-43)

[24] Bill Newman, *The Power of Successful Life,* (Toowong: BNC Publications, 1992) (P.44)

[25] *Bible Illustrator,* (Cedar Rapids, Parsons Technology, 1990)

[26] F Manske, Jr, *Secrets of Effective Leadership,* (Columbia: Leadership Education & Development Inc. 1987) (P.99)